RIDING
FOR MY
LIFE

RIDING
FOR MY
LIFE

JULIE KRONE

with
Nancy Ann Richardson

Little, Brown and Company

BOSTON   NEW YORK   TORONTO   LONDON

First Edition

Library of Congress Cataloging-in-Publication Data
Krone, Julie.
    Riding for my life / Julie Krone with Nancy Ann Richardson. — 1st ed.
        p.   cm.
    ISBN 0-316-50477-7
    1. Krone, Julie.   2. Jockeys — United States — Biography.   3. Women
jockeys — United States — Biography.   I. Richardson, Nancy Ann.
II. Title.
SF336.K76A3   1995
798.4'0092 — dc20
[B]   94-24976

                    10 9 8 7 6 5 4 3 2 1

                              MV–NY

              Published simultaneously in Canada by
              Little, Brown & Company (Canada) Limited

              Printed in the United States of America

CONTENTS

ACKNOWLEDGMENTS

It would be nearly impossible for me to mention, let alone thank, every individual who has positively influenced my life and career. Yet the idea that I might fail to mention friends, colleagues, and loved ones has plagued me throughout the year I've spent writing my story. If it is possible to say a universal thank you, then this is it. With all my heart, thank you for your love, understanding, and support.

Unfortunately, mere words can't convey my thanks to the thousands of horses I have ridden, and the uniquely special ones who have carried me toward the type of success that a kid from Eau Claire, Michigan, used to dream about. For those horses, I hope my actions — the white grapes I bring them for special treats, soft words, gentle pats, and unbridled enthusiasm — somehow convey my love and thanks.

Finally special thanks to my agent, Larry "Snake" Cooper, and my valet, Tony Millan, who have enriched and enhanced both my professional and personal life. And to Chick Lang Jr., whose office I never left without a smile on my face — I will always cherish his memory.

Julie Krone

My thanks to Mom, Dad, and Susan — always. And to Julie, for sharing her life's ride.

Nancy Ann Richardson

A special thanks to Dan Leary of the New York Racing Association for sharing his knowledge of the world of racing and helping in fact checking and research.

J. K. and N. A. R.

RIDING
FOR MY
LIFE

PROLOGUE

My heart burns hard and fast
My mind thinks of impossible things
far and vast
My body craves wild uncontrolled
movement
—JULIE, AGE 13—

I DON'T REMEMBER FALLING. There was the thunderous beat of hooves, wildly swishing tails, and *snap-whack* of sticks, then, instead of horses' ears flattened by the wind and their jockeys' words, a glimpse of the green shrubs that line the racetrack.

On August 30, 1993, in the jockeys' room at Saratoga Race Course, I had been thinking about moving day. Time to pack my trunks and go to Belmont Park to begin another season. As always I was one step behind, which is why Tony Millan, my valet, is indispensable. Tony packs my tack — saddles and pads as well as all my boots, helmets, jockey colors, and other professional gear. That day I was to ride the third race and then the seventh, so I would have time between the races to help Tony pack. I remember I was trying to figure out when to pick up my dry cleaning, whether I should leave that night to beat the traffic or stay until the next morning, what boxes to put in my car, and when to get my cat, Snigglefritz, to my house in New Jersey.

I dressed quickly for the third race and ran out to have a word with Jonathan Sheppard, Seattle Way's trainer. Jonathan told me his filly was big and free-running, and that I needed to be careful not to put Seattle Way in a position that would stop her, because she had trouble getting going again. Then it was time for the race.

The air at the track was electric with the hot breath of barely controlled horses, the announcer's cry of "And they're off!" and the thunder of hooves and heartbeats. There's an excitement at the track that is based to a large degree on danger and the unknown. Professional horse racing is the only sport where an ambulance follows the athletes around the track. The only sport where the gate crew and outriders instinctively count the number of jockeys crossing the finish line, because frequently some jockeys don't get that far. On the morning of August 30, I was one of those jockeys.

I was progressively moving up on the outside, in the clear. Inside of me and to my rear several horses were boxed in — trapped behind my horse, Seattle Way. I remember thinking how clever I was, trapping those horses so they were not in a position to run their fastest. My turn for home was going to be clear; there were no riders in my way. I was fourth or fifth as I rounded the corner, but my position was improving and I had a good chance to win. Then the jockey to my inside, Filiberto Leon, pulled on his right rein and his horse bumped my filly on her shoulder. She stumbled.

There was a flash of sound and color, jumbled together in a single moment. Then I was spinning, riding the air instead of Seattle Way. I landed on my ankle, but I had no chance to lie still and check the damage. The momentum of my fall sent me tumbling again. In midair, my vision caught the blur of a horse moving toward me. I was very aware that the horse was going to strike me. I'm going to be killed, I thought. Then Two Is Trouble, all twelve hundred pounds of him, struck me in the chest. It felt like a powerful push, not a good sharp strike, because I was wearing a two-pound Tipperary brand flak jacket made of high-density foam. The blow sent me through the air, folding at the hips, heels over head in a whiplash action. Then there was nothing. No horses, no thunder, no whirlwind of color. Just the dry turf under my back, and pain.

It's all spoiled. That was my first thought. There are only sixty-one jockeys in the United States who have won three thousand races. That was my private goal before my fall at Saratoga. I had already started counting how many wins I needed at Saratoga and Belmont. I figured that I was going to win about five races a week at every meet. I even had a date planned when I was going to win my three thousandth race. It was all spoiled.

I didn't even try to move. After a fall I usually wriggle the body parts I think are hurt to figure out how bad it is. But this time I couldn't move my upper torso, my right ankle, or my left arm, which was sliced open with the elbow joint exposed. I just lay on the turf, exactly as I'd come to rest, my right leg bent, my left arm out to the side. All I wanted was my goggles off. I slowly raised my right arm and removed them. I thought about how comforting it would have been to have fallen face down in cool, soft dirt instead of on my back on hard turf. Then there were people surrounding me, voices, and hot licks of pain that turned to lightning.

The bones in my ankle were broken so badly that when I grabbed my foot, it rotated around until the heel faced me. I screamed and turned my foot back. Everyone was talking at once. "Should we move her?" "Don't move her." "Wait for the paramedics." The ambulance pulled up. After assessing my condition, one of the paramedics decided that he needed to cut off my boot to stabilize my ankle. "Don't touch it! Don't touch it!" I screamed. He wouldn't listen. The skin on my ankle was so torn and punctured that it wasn't even skin anymore, and the paramedic kept gouging into the area with his scissors in an attempt to get my boot off. Finally he noticed that I was in respiratory trouble — I later learned that I had a cardiac contusion from the blow — and dropped the scissors.

I'm not a doctor, and I don't really know what the right or wrong procedures are, but darned if that paramedic didn't try to cut off my boot again once he'd put me on oxygen. I was in such excruciating pain that I wasn't able to look up at the guy and say, "Pal, take those scissors and put them in your pocket." He wasn't saving my life by cutting my boot off. He was just hurting me more. That paramedic's job was to stabilize me enough to get me to the hospital, that's all. Finally Tony Millan, my valet, stopped him, and they decided to load me into the ambulance and take me to the Saratoga hospital.

I screamed bloody murder when they moved me. I could feel my bones crunching. The ride to the hospital was excruciating. Tony and two officials from the track rode with me.

Tony held my hand, kept everyone away from my ankle, adjusted the oxygen, and desperately tried to make me more comfortable. There wasn't much he could do. Everyone tried to distract me with stories about horses and races, but nothing worked. The pain was so wrenching that if someone had held a gun to my head and asked if I wanted him to shoot me, I would have considered the offer.

– 1 –

FILLY

WHEN I WAS five years old, I killed a horse. His name was Ibn, and he died two days after a car struck him in the middle of the road that ran by our home in Coloma, Michigan.

It was my fault. The night before Ibn was hit, I had gone out to feed and water the horses. I was so afraid of the dark that when I ran back into the house, I forgot to stop and make sure the gate had clicked shut. It hadn't, and Ibn wandered out onto the road and was struck. My mother only told me one time that I had killed that pony. After that, she left it alone. But I couldn't leave it alone. For months I cried for Ibn, and for my part in his death.

Ibn was the first baby horse that I trained with my mother. Mom taught me all the ways to introduce a young horse to bridle and saddle, and how to train a horse to want to please a rider, which ultimately creates a positive experience for both horse and rider. When I'd climb down the steps of my school bus after classes, Ibn would whinny to me from the pasture. I would race for the barn, my books purposely left behind at school, and begin my true education — the training of horses. There was a wonderful bond between me and Ibn, and my mother was with us every step of the way to make sure I learned my lessons well. To lose an animal I had worked so hard on was devastating. To lose my friend was heartrending. Even after my first pony, Dixie, had Filly — whom I named Ibn Fernie's Madih (Madih means "favorite one" in Arabic) and called Filly for short — my sense of guilt about Ibn remained.

Soon after the birth of Filly, our family — Mom, Dad, my older brother, Donnie, and I — moved to Eau Claire, Michigan, to the farm that would eventually house most of my childhood memories. As we pulled into the drive, the first thing I saw was the maple tree. It was the biggest tree I had seen in all six years of my life. The limbs stretched out fifteen feet from the massive trunk and were so wide that I could literally run across them. Soon there would be a ladder that would lean from its largest extending branch and a tire swing that would hang from another of its generous arms. The beautifully manicured lawn would become a muddy tract from the constant scuff of our bare feet. I didn't know it that first day, but that tree would become my world, a dinner table, boat, space ship, refuge.

I remember my early childhood in Eau Claire. Sunlit days spent with the Wolske kids, Debbie, Matt, and Kathy, racing our ponies, skinny-dipping in swimming holes, and picking handfuls of sweet purple berries from the bushes. Every other spare moment was spent with my brother, Donnie, Tracey

Hanner, and the Garland boys, Kenny, Tommy, and Mark, eating green apples, playing cowboys and Indians and tackle football. Even then I was as athletic and powerful as the boys.

It was my mother's dream that her children have a fantasy childhood, filled with animals, friends, and country fun. There were no fences to keep us in, no locked doors, rules, or set mealtimes. I was as wild as the animals on the farm, and just as free. There were times when my mother came under fire from the neighbors for allowing me that freedom. But even if she had tried to impose rules, I would not have followed them. She understood that because she understood my nature.

During those early days, I had several animal companions. Gretta, a Saint Bernard, a Great Dane named Arrow, Ben, a long-haired Siamese cat, and Filly, my pony. Gretta was an enormous dog, the last of the Saint Bernards my mother had bred. She used to grab the rope attached to my tire swing with her teeth and pull the swing as far back as possible before letting me fly. The trip up through the air was wonderful, but I always knew I was in trouble on the downswing. Gretta's favorite game was to swing me forward and then lunge at the tire when I came back, knocking me into the mud. While I was at school Gretta occupied herself by walking our colts in the yard. She'd grab their dangling lead ropes and prance around the farmhouse, the colts trotting happily behind her. But the minute my school bus arrived, she'd drop everything.

When I was seven, I truly believe that Gretta thought I was one of her puppies. When the school bus dropped me off, I'd walk the fifteen feet from the dirt road to our fence, climb the fence, and walk another ten feet to my tree, and that was usually as far as I'd get. Gretta would come bounding toward me, her brown and white tail flying and her enormous mouth wide open. She'd chomp onto my jacket and drag me through the yard to the back door, then lie down and begin to lick the mud and dirt off my clothes as if she were cleaning one of her own pups. I would cry because I couldn't get out from under her huge paws. Arrow was just as big as Gretta, but much easier for me to handle. In the winter I'd hook her up to my sled and we'd mush through the snow-covered streets.

My cat, Ben, was a particular favorite, because he'd walk me to the school bus every morning and meet me each afternoon. Ben would leave my side only when Gretta bounded toward me. I didn't blame him — I would have run away, too, if I had been fast enough.

I loved Arrow and Ben, but most of my time was spent with my pony, Filly. Half Arab, half Shetland, and one hundred percent diabolical, she was my constant companion. Together we learned how to become a knowledgeable rider and an educated pony. The education was neither smooth nor easy. To this day, however, I credit Filly with teaching me to ride well. Just by being her nasty self, she taught me more than any other horse or instructor.

Filly was elusive, naughty, and at times downright mean. In the beginning, if I wanted to put the bridle on her, I couldn't catch her. If I tied her to a fence, she'd chew through the rope and get loose. And when I rode her, she would constantly plot ways to buck me off. Sometimes Filly would get so angry with me for trying to train her that she would throw herself on the ground or sit back on her hind legs and then jump into the air and take off bucking. My mom was usually there to help, but sometimes Filly and I just had to work things out on our own.

There were times when I'd be five miles away from home and she would grab the side of the bridle in her teeth and just run off. My mother would pass us in the truck, and I'd wave at her and smile as Filly ran away with me.

I used to wrap a T-shirt around my saddle horn and whip it out to put over Filly's eyes to slow her down. Sometimes it worked, but it also backfired. One time I put the shirt over her eyes and Filly kept running until we went clattering right over the well pit — a deep hole with old wood stacked over the top. Why that well pit didn't fall in, I'll never know. My mother saw the whole thing from the window and couldn't believe we made it over. At other times Filly would race for the barn door, not caring that I was still on her back, and I'd have to leap off to avoid being decapitated.

Everything I did with Filly was an experiment. But by experimenting I learned to ride instinctively. There are some things a rider has to learn by touch, by reaction — lessons no instructor can give. I learned what a horse does when he crosses a creek, or a bridge where planks are missing; and what happens when you come upon a bush with a bird that suddenly jumps out; or when a pheasant races along your pathway and then spreads its wings and takes off right in front of your horse's face. Those were all new experiences for Filly and me. We managed to conquer the bridges and creeks, but the birds took longer. Several times Filly bucked, twisting sideways until she had me off her back, and took off down the trail. There I'd be, twelve miles from home without a horse. It only took a few long walks home before I realized that when I was riding, I had to be ready for anything. And once I had mastered Filly's stubborn nature, she performed and reacted ten times better than other ponies in similar situations.

Racehorses are very spirited and skittish and can never be counted on to act consistently, but I am always ready for a sideways duck or a buck. It's just a natural instinct now. All those summers riding bareback on Filly by myself in the woods, with nothing but a bridle, a pair of shorts, and no shoes, gave me an incredible education.

It's hard to explain in words what I learned from Filly. It's like asking an ice-skater how they do a triple. They can say, Well, I jump in the air as high as I can, I point my toes, my arms go up, I try to keep my hips tight — but it's impossible to explain the entire physical action. If someone were to ask me how I keep a horse from lugging in (pulling hard to one side), I would answer that there are many different things I do, that every fifth of a second I'm changing my movements to make the horse work correctly. Or, if someone wanted to know how I make a horse bow, well, I could get on a horse and make him bow, but the way I do it depends on how much rock and give (flexibility and movement) the horse has and if it gives (reacts to my cues) right away. If it's a horse that's in between, then I have to be soft and not demand too much right away; and if he gets tired of my instruction and begins to fight, I have to change my strategy again. That's what Filly taught me — to go beyond training a horse to walk, trot, and canter. To understand and respect a horse's "depth."

To this day, Filly is the deepest, most conniving, trickiest horse I've ever known. In those early days she was so bad that my mother said she was going to look around for another pony.

Mom hated to watch my frustration, but even then she knew that I'd already fallen in love with Filly and that her words would just fill me with more grit and determination — which was really her plan. Filly just fought everything; she fought setting her head, carrying herself in a balanced manner, accepting the bit and leg at the same time so she was between my hands and legs. But I wouldn't give up and let my mom sell her, because I was determined to accomplish something with her. I had to work doubly hard to get Filly to the point where I could show her. But in the long run, that work paid off, and I could win almost any class with her. Dressage — precision riding, using hand and leg aids and the horse's flexion and balance — is the most demanding kind of riding, and Filly and I won those classes, too.

Eight years after leaving home to become a jockey, I began to have dreams about Filly, dreams that she was in danger or trouble and that she needed me. When I had grown out of my pony, my mother sold her to a neighboring farm, so I called home to see if she remembered the name of Filly's new owner. My mom said that Filly had changed hands from the original purchaser, and that she didn't know who had her. I called every barn in Michigan. "Have you seen a dark gray pony named Ibn Fernie's Madih?" I asked hundreds of times. Finally I traced Filly to the last barn on my list. "No, we don't have a pony by the name Ibn, Fernie, or Madih," the woman on the line said. "No pony named Filly?" I asked in desperation. "Oh, Filly, sure we have her, but we're just about to take her to an auction." "I want to buy her," I said quickly. "Don't sell her, I'll be there in two days."

I drove a four-cylinder truck from New Jersey to Michigan.

When I arrived at the barn, the owner — still unsure why I wanted to buy an old pony, but more than willing to part with her — took me out to the field where Filly was tied. As the woman directed me to her, my heart sank. It wasn't my pony. My pony was dark gray, and this one was pure white. But as I approached, I saw that it was Filly, just many years older.

"Don't get on her. She'll buck you off. She bucks everyone off," the owner warned. I untied Filly, threw my lead rope around her neck, and jumped on her bare back. She was like a machine — she remembered everything, all her tricks. The owner was speechless as I loaded my pony into the horse trailer. I paid five hundred dollars for Filly, but I would have paid fifty thousand. She was my pony, and we were going home.

Every half hour during the drive back from Michigan to New Jersey, I stopped to pick Filly a five-gallon bucket of grass. I could tell that she didn't feel well, and when I took her temperature it was a bit high. The grass helped keep Filly's system working. Horses have specialized digestive tracts, adapted to diets containing large quantities of plant fiber. "Shipping sickness" is common with horses because of the stress involved in moving them. They can develop coughs or become colicky or feverish. The grass I fed Filly helped the passage of food through her intestines and prevented additional discomfort. And, since the leading cause of death in horses is colic, many times the result of poor parasite control, too little fiber, and not enough feeding frequency, the grass was very important. Filly was pretty stressed to begin with, so I had to take extra care in shipping her home. The first night on the road I stopped at a motel and backed the truck up to my room's door. I wanted to be sure that no one bothered Filly during the night.

The following morning I discovered that Filly wasn't drinking enough water. Once again, the stress of the trip was taking its toll. Filly was becoming dehydrated — horses need to drink at least five gallons of water a day — so I soaked a hay bag in my shower and hung it in the back of the truck. Filly began to eat the hay. I was relieved. At least she was getting some fluids. For the next twenty-four hours we continued to stop for grass and water. It was a long trip, but worth every bit of work. As I rounded the last corner to the farm where I would board her, we passed a little white church. Its bells began to ring, and Filly whinnied along with the bells. At the age of eighteen, she knew she was home.

I had plans for my pony. First, she had a full physical from the vet, was medicated, wormed, and jugged (given an injection of fluids and vitamins). The vet X-rayed her feet and discovered that she had acute laminitis, a hoof disease that can be detrimental to a horse's soundness if not detected early and can cause death if not cured. It took almost a month to get Filly back into shape, but I had the time — it was 1989 and I was still recuperating from a spill in which I had badly broken my arm. When she was finally fit, I called my friends the Freundlichs and asked them to come to the farm where Filly was being boarded.

There is a saying that friendship can't be bought. It's not always true. My best friends, Paula and Pete Freundlich and their daughters, Krista and Stefanie, had "bought" me as a dinner companion at a Monmouth Park charity auction for four hundred dollars. Their daughter Krista was only about two years old at the time. I had waved to Krista one day at the track, and she'd told me her name. The next day Krista and her parents were there again, and I said, "Hi, Krista." She couldn't believe I remembered her — so she fell in love with me. After that first dinner I fell in love with the entire Freundlich family.

The next year at the charity auction, I begged the Freundlichs to buy me again. I was more expensive, around a thousand dollars, but they bought me anyway. The things your friends will do for you! The Freundlichs are a warm and loving family, and when I am on the road we all write letters and send pictures to each other. They were the reason I knew exactly what to do with my pony.

The Freundlichs accepted my invitation to the farm, so that morning I washed Filly, and when her long white mane had been combed until it was silk, I wove pink and violet wildflowers through her mane and tail. Then I made a crown of flowers and placed it on her head along with a blue silk halter. When Paula, Pete, and the girls arrived, I led them out to the barn. "This is Filly," I said as I opened her stall door, "and she's for you." Krista and Steffi, who were six and four at the time, were speechless. Filly looked so gentle and beautiful, her snow-white body covered with wildflowers, her white forelock stirring in the breeze. I led her out of the stall, hopped on her back, and showed the Freundlich family all her tricks — bowing, answering yes and no, sitting like a dog, counting, and mounting a block.

"Don't be misled by this pony," I warned as she performed flawlessly. "She is a diabolical creature inside, full of spit and nasty thoughts. If you girls can learn to ride Filly, to beat her at her own games, then you'll be able to ride any horse in the world. She's a rotten little pony, a master of deviousness, but if you learn how to ride her, she'll respect you, be your best friend, and always take care of you. And once you master her she'll perform better than any other pony. There's a marvelous side to Filly, but you'll have to work hard to find it."

It was wonderful to give the Freundlich girls something that meant so much to me, because *they* mean so much to me. They took Filly home in 1990. They still have her, and both girls are becoming very knowledgeable riders. I had it easier than they do. Filly and I were educated at the same time. Today she knows how to do everything, and that makes her even trickier to ride. Filly's life has truly come full circle from the time I was a child. She is once again winning trail classes, ridden both English and western style, and speed classes, and Paula drives her in front of a beautiful cart.

I still visit Filly. She lives twenty minutes from my home in New Jersey in a barn beside the Freundlichs' house with three other ponies. Filly has changed the family's life. And I am constantly amazed at her spunk and her capacity to perform (at age twenty-four) at a higher level than other show ponies. The girls' rooms now look like mine did as a child — walls covered with blue, red, yellow, and pink ribbons, shelves stacked with all the glistening trophies they've won. It is more than likely that someday Filly will be responsible for helping them realize their dreams, just as she helped me realize my own.

– 2 –

BEST FRIENDS

THE DAY MY family arrived in Eau Claire, Michigan, we found a little girl named Tracey Hanner sitting on the boxes in our living room. It was as if she came with the house. And although she was younger by three years, we became blood sisters and were inseparable. Tracey was one of those rare childhood friends who can never be forgotten or replaced — she was my buddy, confidante, and partner in crime.

We spent the days pushing our bodies to the limit — leaping off the corners of the barn in rough-and-tumble games, racing through the forest on black and white ponies or dirty brown feet, and spending hours in my special tree, cloaked by the dark green leaves. We relished the heat of noonday sun, the numbing cold of bubbling creekwater, and the scratch of branches on bare legs. In the winter we jumped from mountains of snow, mushed my dog attached to a sled over crunching white streets, and built fantastic snow forts. Those years were filled with simple joys, the pure happiness that comes from not understanding the grown-up world and not having to understand.

Tracey and I smoked our first cigarette together and had the same scab on our knees from crashing our bikes, a scab we would pick until identical droplets of blood appeared. We had a lot in common, but there was a wild streak in me that was not as evident in Tracey, and though I never meant to get her in trouble, I invariably did. Her parents were strict, and mine, well, I could do just about anything I pleased. My father, a junior high school art teacher and photographer, spent his days teaching and his evenings hidden in his darkroom. When my mother wasn't working she was busy with the animals and had no interest in imposing any rules or restrictions on Donnie and me. "No fences for my children," she would always say. But Tracey's parents had curfews, set mealtimes, and punishments for offenses. Still, I spent as much time as possible at the Hanners', always trying to be included in dinners, and making Tracey's mother feel guilty if she sent me home to eat a peanut butter sandwich in my tree instead of allowing me to eat at her table.

Tracey had a set bedtime, something I had never experienced. In the evenings the Hanners would send me home, and I'd leave through the front door and wait until Tracey's light went out, then climb through her window. We'd lie under the covers, giggling and talking all night. If we heard her parents coming, I'd hide beneath the bed and then climb out the window later and go home. I was never caught sneaking from Tracey's house, but there were many other times when my actions got her into trouble. It always upset me when Tracey was punished. She was such a sweet, wonderful kid, and I always thought she should have been allowed more freedom. When she was spanked for coming home late and missing her curfew, I suffered with her. I was not immune to punishments. However, mine came at odd times, lasted a bit too long, and were fueled by a frustration and anger that I was incapable of comprehending. Still, those punishments were followed by hugs. My parents were always big huggers. There was a lot of love in my house — you sometimes just had to turn your head sideways to see it.

If there is one special time I remember most with Tracey, it is the Berrien County Fair, the biggest summer fair in the Midwest. All the 4-H clubs are there with horses, goats, rabbits, cows, and home-grown produce. Our 4-H club's name was the Road Runners (it still exists today), reflecting our wild summer days spent running our ponies up and down the roads. A 4-H club is not only a team of kids dedicated to learning about farming and the care and training of animals but also a group of best friends who work extremely hard and have a large dose of pride in themselves and their accomplishments. Midwestern kids take enormous pride in every product they enter in competition, from their onions and green beans to their livestock. The kids work all summer for that one week of the fair, and winning is the ultimate honor. But it's not just the competition, it's the entire atmosphere of music and magic. There are stands along an enormous "midway" with lemonade, cotton candy, and fluorescent-colored T-shirts to buy. For a midwestern farm kid, it's probably the biggest, most exciting event of the year.

When I was five years old I began to compete in riding

classes at the fair. I had a lot of success over the next four years, and it was only natural that I wanted my friend Tracey to share in that success. Tracey was a good rider, and I convinced her to enter a horsemanship class at the fair in 1972. I was determined that she was going to win a ribbon, which is very difficult since each class has up to twenty-five competitors.

For months before the fair began, Tracey came to my house each day for riding lessons. She was a good rider, but she needed work if she was to ribbon in her class. Her biggest difficulty was getting her horse to switch leads (in the canter, the foreleg extending farthest forward in the direction of a turn is the "lead"). He would only take the correct lead in one direction. My mom and I taught Tracey to make her horse buck by hitting him in the rump with her hand, because when a horse bucks, he changes leads. When the time for the county fair arrived, Tracey was ready.

It was dawn when we drove to the fairgrounds. The fog hung in gray sheets, and the road was black and slick with dew. Droplets of weak morning light dripped from the trees as Tracey and I sat silently in the truck. My mother drove through the darkness up a long hill, silent, too, in anticipation of the fair, which meant as much to her as it did to us. Just when the fairgrounds were in sight, the sunlight broke through the fog, and it was almost like entering heaven. I told my mom to drive faster — I was eager to get to heaven.

When it was time for Tracey's horsemanship class, Mom and I hung on the rail and shouted instructions as she entered the ring. Tracey walked, trotted, and cantered in one direction. "Look at the judge!" I yelled. It's important to make some eye contact with the judge, not too much, but enough to know if you're doing everything right. The judge told the riders to switch direction, and Tracey walked and trotted well, but began her canter on the wrong lead. As she passed me, just moments before she came into view of the judge, Tracey made her horse buck, he switched leads, and she rode straight and tall past the judge. The class ended and all twenty-five of the kids lined up for their ribbons. I will never forget how proud we felt when the judge pinned Tracey's horse with a second-place ribbon. We had done it. When she rode out of the ring and dismounted, Mom, Tracey, and I fell into each other's arms, laughing and crying. The sense of love and accomplishment we felt was overwhelming.

Years later, Tracey fell in love with her high school sweetheart and got married. She finished high school pregnant, but still on the honor roll. I couldn't even get through high school, and she was married, pregnant, and still doing well. Sometimes she just amazed me. When I left for Tampa Bay Downs to become a jockey, Tracey had just given birth to a son. I called her all the time, and she'd tell me about her husband, Doug, and their son, and I'd tell her about becoming a jockey.

At Christmastime, 1993, I went to visit Tracey. There was light snow on the ground, and it crunched under my feet as I walked slowly to her grave. The headstone was gray-and-rose-colored marble, and the weak winter sunlight glanced off its carved letters. I withdrew a long love note that I had written on the plane, and placed it on her grave along with some mistletoe, so she and Doug could kiss. They're buried next to each other, with their unborn child. They died in a motorcycle accident —

Doug was killed instantly and Tracey was in a coma for some time before she passed away. At the time of her death, she was pregnant with her second child.

I hadn't seen her in several years, and was riding in Maryland when the telephone call came: "I know Tracey would want you to know . . . she's dead." I refused to accept that my childhood friend was gone. I didn't go to the funeral, didn't write her parents a note until the following year.

Before I went to Tracey's grave, I met with her parents. I told them how much I missed her and how much I still loved her. I met Tracey's beautiful son, Jason, who lives with her parents. It is such a loss for him that he will never truly know his mother. After Tracey's death, the Hanner's house burned down, so almost all of their photos and remembrances of Tracey are gone, too. That's another tragedy for them, and for Jason. Following my visit, I went to Tracey's grave and read my letter to her. I sat there for hours and cried for us all.

To this day, I can't smell popcorn without thinking of Tracey. I still keep her telephone number in my phone book. Even if I lose my book or get a new one, I transfer her number. Everyone has a way of remembering someone they love. I guess that's mine.

– 3 –

LEARNING TO FLY

WHEN WE WERE eleven years old, my other best friend, Lori Probst, and I discovered a map that showed that the railroad tracks in Michigan traversed the entire country. We decided that what we were going to do for the rest of our lives was walk the tracks, eating by stealing fruit from all the orchards along the way. We began to practice, packing a Baggie full of grapes and venturing seven or eight miles down the rails until we were too tired to continue walking and turned for home. Eleven-year-olds walking eight miles, passing seedy areas populated by hobos who called to us and sometimes followed us for miles — when I think now of Lori's little girl, Rachel, doing what we did, I shudder. But we didn't care. All we wanted to do was escape.

Lori and I were friends from the time my family moved to Eau Claire, but not in the same way that Tracey and I were friends. It wasn't just that we had brothers who took childhood games and taunting and perfected them to fine art. We both came from families where the pressures of marriage were tearing apart the tenuous seams of our lives.

I taught Lori how to fly. It was more than twenty feet from the peak of our barn to the dirt below. Not hay, dirt. Leaping twenty feet and landing in a crumple of skin and bones truly felt like flying. There's a moment of suspension before the stomach lurches to the throat and threatens to escape from a screaming mouth. That moment is ecstasy. Lori lived in town with her stepfather and a mother who wanted her to act like a lady. She lived in a body that began to bloom early, and had a face that drew boys and men before she even knew what they wanted. Spending time at our farm, learning how to be free, was part of her escape. And just being with Lori was part of mine.

Just as I taught Lori how to fly, she taught me how to walk with my feet on the ground. She was the first to tell me when I got carried away — she drew the parental line for me in the sand. Still, sometimes nothing could stop me from expressing the frustration and rage that erupted from my soul. I used to beat boys up — never girls, just boys. Lori and I would go to a football game, and I'd look over at her and say, "I'll be back, I've got to go beat someone up." I felt like the boys all thought they were so cool, and it was my job to straighten them out. But Lori understood my anger. None of the boys paid attention to me, the little runt. "Love them, don't fight with them," Lori would call out as I left the grandstand. "Okay, if you have to fight, be careful, and fight hard," she'd add, acknowledging that she couldn't stop me. On my way, I'd gather a posse of younger girls and boys so that I'd have a gang with me when I found my victim. I rarely lost.

Still, Lori and I never found total escape from our lives. Drugs were the closest we ever came. I can't remember when we began to smoke pot, but I'd guess we were around twelve years old. We stole — fifty cents from our mothers' purses, a stray joint from our brothers' rooms. But there were no consequences to our actions. Lori and I skipped school, sometimes went to classes high — nobody paid attention. Our parents were immersed in their own lives, their own troubles. And we weren't doing it for attention. We just wanted to forget our families, our lives.

And what about our teachers? They didn't seem to notice either. I remember being stoned in my high school English class and laughing uncontrollably during a video about vowels and nouns. "I am a noun," a little blue cartoon creature said as it danced across the screen. I thought the film was hilarious. My teacher turned off the projector, flicked on the lights, and said, "Julie, please make yourself conspicuous by your absence." I'll never forget that. He didn't care what was going on with me, he just wanted me to leave the room because I was disruptive.

The only reason I went to school at all was to attend gym and Mr. Down's art class. The opportunity to express myself on canvas in magenta, purple, emerald green, and blood red, and to be told that those expressions were not only good, but some of the best work he'd ever seen, was the only thing that kept me in school. Mr. Down didn't know that I was doing drugs once in a while, but he knew that I needed some positive feedback from an adult. And he knew there was something boiling inside me that had to be expressed. But after his second period class, I'd head to the parking lot to find Lori. Then I'd return to school to attend gym class. Even then I was a strong athlete, and Mrs. Valentine's gym class was a big part of my life. Mr. Down, gym, my animals, Tracey, and Lori, that was all that mattered, because that was all that made me feel worth more than a pile of beans. Those things, and my dream to become a jockey, which Lori knew of and wholeheartedly supported.

She has always supported my dreams, and I have always supported hers. Lori's heart's desire was to become a wife and mother. She was still in high school when she met her future husband, who was many years her senior and already had a son. But she knew what she wanted with a maturity and certainty that made her decision to marry Ray Skinner and become the mother of his son, Josh, the right one. And it is a decision she has never regretted.

Lori and I both had dreams, and we both made them happen, something that ties us together. That bond enabled us to leave the difficulties of our childhoods behind and visit them only when we feel strong.

Last year I was watching *The Exorcist* on television and called Lori during a commercial. "Turn it off," she commanded. I did. Lori knows what will upset me, just as she knows when I'm on the phone before she picks up the line, and I know when she needs me and always call at the right time. There is a tie between us that stretches across the miles when we are apart. And we live through each other. Lori is a wife and mom. Her husband, Ray, and children, Josh and Rachel, are a family, and whether I'm with them or far away, I'm part of that family. Just as when I'm riding, Lori is on that horse, too. When she watched me win the Belmont Stakes, Lori said she actually felt like she was riding the race with me. She smelled the horses and felt the vibration of hooves as we tore down the stretch. She had cramps in her thighs when the race was over.

Lori Probst Skinner and Julie Krone are part of each other. Not just because we shared our childhoods, but because we each live inside the other, in a place apart from the hurt and desperation. It's a beautiful place where we can always go, because it's home.

– 4 –

THE JOURNAL

A TATTERED YELLOW journal, with "Julie" drawn across the cover in red, green, and black, sits in my childhood trunk. The metal spiral that holds the worn sheets together has rusted, bleeding orange stains onto the edge of each lined page. But the journal remains intact, and tells the story of the fourteenth year of my life, 1977–78, the year of my first love and my parents' angry divorce.

That year I found solace in animals, sports, fights, and the release of writing stories and poems that mirrored my life. My journal was part of the homework assigned by my ninth grade English teacher, Miss Shilling. I hated writing in a journal. My handwriting was never as neat as I wanted, and figuring out what to write was always a dilemma. It is only as an adult, looking back over those pages filled with stories, poems, loves, confusion, and anger, that I realize the importance of that journal and the value of having a place and a person with whom to share my thoughts. There were many long nights when I turned to the journal to express my feelings, and to Miss Shilling's comments, written in green pen in the margin by my entries, for reassurance that what I felt had been acknowledged, had mattered.

9-28-77 Hi Miss Shilling sorry I can't print — have to write in cursive — YUCK! I hate writing, it is so hard. If I were a horse I wouldn't have to do something so dumb. Chuck won homecoming King I nominated him. I like him a lot. — *Julie*

10-6-77 Chuck called me last night and asked me who I'm going to the dance with. I thought right there he was going to ask me — oh wow! Then he said I don't know who I'm going to go with. I felt like hanging up on him but instead I talked to him for about a half hour.

I like him more and more all the time I see him or talk to him. I wrote a real gushy letter and I think he liked it. He has terrible hand writing and I wonder sometimes how come I like him so much he's really not that super but he's awful cute. I guess I just like him I wish he would go back out with me. (I think I love him — Julie + Chuck) — *Julie*

MISS SHILLING: There's no accounting for taste.

10-7-77 Chuck still didn't tell me who he is going to take to the dance it makes me mad. I'm gonna climb the walls I like him even more today than yesterday. I really think I love him he's a pretty sweet guy and he's cute but that doesn't always count but it doesn't hurt either (I love Chuck!) — *Julie*

10-9-77 Chuck and I went to the dance together — fun, fun, fun! But I don't feel like I love him any more. I guess its cause he was being a brat today — *Julie*

10-31-77 Miss Shilling that was not nice not letting me go to the bathroom. I'm really mad at you I think you should be more tollerable of us and let us go to the bathroom and get a drink. You were down right mean. How would you like it if someone was to have an accident, it would be all your fault. I would be ashamed of myself if I were you. — *Julie*

11-7-77 I don't feel like writing a story today. I'm not in a funny mood and when I'm not in a funny mood the story turns out very dumb. I'll write it afterwords, when we come back from thanksgiving. A writer can't write two pages of a story and make it good if she's not in the mood so I'll just write big and sloppy and fill up the paper like this — *Julie*

MISS SHILLING: Everyone has an off day now and then.

11-30-77 I'm mad because I don't feel good. I have a stuffy nose and watery eyes and I'm confused. I have to fill up this whole page and I don't know what to write. I have a lot of things to say but I can't tell you because they are too personal and the stuff is really not mine to tell. Oh I'm so bored. I wish I had a worm right now. I would tear it up in little shreds because I'm so mad. It would not hurt him because worms don't have feelings. Sometimes I get in the mood to punch someone's face or run as fast as I can for a mile — *Julie*

MISS SHILLING: I'm glad you don't have a worm. How do you know they don't have feelings? They don't wiggle on a fish-hook because it tickles!

12-2-77 Sometimes Miss Shilling you can be mean. You said I could ask people if they believed in Capital Punishment and then you yelled at me and imbarressed the crap out of me and made me sit down. It is not fair you aren't even as understanding as you used to be. You gave me a headache. I felt like crying. I hate that when people say one thing and don't mean it. I think you did it on purpose — *Julie*

MISS SHILLING: Julie I did not yell at you on purpose. Please look at my side. With twenty kids all wanting something different every hour of every day, sometimes I lose my perspective. Have a heart. I never said I was perfect.

1-8-78 Hi there Miss Shilling, what are you going for, this weeks grouchie teacher of the year award, or was it your new years resolution to be meaner to your students. I know how you work now. If you start out the class nice, your gonna end mean, and if you start out mean, you'll end nice. You probably get up out of your bed every morning and decide which it'll be. — *Julie*

MISS SHILLING: Yup.

1-10-78 I really messed up my test Miss Shilling. I wish I wouldn't have I really wanted to pass I studied but I just forgot. I know how to do it, I really do. I did a test at home with my dad and I got most of the questions right. It really scares me cause I forgot — *Julie*

MISS SHILLING: How did you forget . . . what parts?

1-12-78 What Miss Shilling is to me when I'm mad — ugly stupid farty, ruthless, cruel, idiodic, a thief, a wiredo a dummy, lippy nappy puss faced fat, untolerant, pickleface burrhead, a nag, scaggy greedy a crab wichie mouthy, bosy, dumb too, boring, a poop shoot — *Julie*

MISS SHILLING: Julie, I wish you'd learn how to spell!

1-13-78 You're my english teacher, you're supposed to teach me how to spell!

2-10-78 Well hello there Miss Shilling. I went to bed at six thirty last night and didn't get up all night — oh I take that back, I did get up cause I had this weird craving for some water so I got my glass and I started across the room and tripped over the fan. Then I went looking for the door handle and slammed right into the door — WOW! did that hurt. Then, after hurting my self a little bit more I finally got to the bathroom and I was getting ready to walk into the bathroom and I stepped on the dog and fell into the tub. And wouldn't you know it, there was water in it cause my mom dried some clothes that day. What a night! I went back upstairs and I even forgot my water! That's why I've got bruises today — *Julie*

2-20-78 A poem for you —

I once had a friend
who lived in a tree
he'd unzipped his pants cause he had to go pee

He'd pee on the roots
down beneath this great place
like a cloud dropping water
Like a star dropping space

He'd laugh and he'd giggle
when it fell to the ground
like a jolly old man
with a friendly little sound

This place in the forest
built of nothing but wood
to him was a palace
only he understood

His furniture was broken
and his clothes they were ripped
his shoes they were torn
and his fausetts they dripped

But he loved what he did
and did what he loved
he fed his fury little animals
the fish and the doves

Now pepole you may laugh
at the man in the tree
and think that his life was shere misery

There's no one around
except for his friends
a rabbit a squirrel
and a deer he calls Ben

The man lived there
since he was a kid
but he kinda died last summer
oh yes he sure did!

They say there's a heaven
we go when we die
far beyond the clouds
way deep in the sky
the place that we'll live
when we're old and die

But the man in the tree
on the scale up to seven
came back to the tree
for it was his heaven

He still lives so happy
with a belly full of joy
in his old wooden home
where he lived as a boy

So if you ever hear a laugh and a giggle if you should
it's probably the old man in his home full of wood.
— Julie —

MISS SHILLING: This story is really cute. I like your rhyming —
shows some thought. How come you don't show all this in-
telligence in class?

2-21-78 What do you mean by that? I show a lot of intelli-
gence in class, you just never catch it cause it comes and goes
so fast.

2-25-78 People make me sick Miss Shilling. This day has
been worse than any day in my life. I just felt like a fool all day.
You know it started this morning in math. Keith was sitting in
my seat and Diane Barrow was sitting in his and Mrs. Goldner
screamed, I mean literally screamed at me to sit down. Imbar-
est the shit out of me.

Then I went to gym and we played kickball and Butch Price
and Paul Mattel and those other guys played the whole game
and wouldn't let anybody else play. Then I went to speech
class. Everybody knew that I was gonna do a speech to make
people laugh so they got together and no one laughed. I felt so
dumb. I felt like killing them. I'm really serious — literally
killing them.

Oh Miss Shilling, I felt a frog in my throat all day. You know,
one of those crying kinds. My mom and dad's divorce came in
final and now all they do is fight over everything. This morning
they fought over the round oak table. We have two of them but
they fought anyway. We might have to move. For some reason
I feel dizzy and sick *— Julie*

3-2-78 I found out why Miss Hudson is quiting. She doesn't feel like she belongs here. She likes the kids and all, its just that her family is in Kalamazoo and she wants to go to a place where she can fit in real good. Miss Shilling you ought to tell her though that she can never turn back to the good old days

   — Julie

5-25-78 Hello Miss Shilling. I can't believe that my freshman class is done and over with. In three more years I won't even be in school. I'm still a little kid though. Maybe I just don't want to grow up and have the responsability of a grown up. Well, I'm sure gonna miss you over the sommer (what some pepole will say — haha!). No really, I'm gonna miss you *— Bye, Julie*

− 5 −

THE GAME NOBODY WINS

When my parents decided to get divorced, they made a list of all their belongings and divided them in two. My father's photography equipment was an even trade with my mother's horse stuff. The furniture, pictures, clocks and kitchenware were split. They even fought over my bedroom set. When I heard that, I wanted to smash everything in my room. What were they planning to do with *me?* Split me in half and each take a portion? When parents divorce, that's what happens to their children. They are forced to stay in one place while a part of them is torn away, and they are powerless to affect the situation.

> *I feel bad real bad. Not physically*
> *mently. She doesn't like him. He likes*
> *her. He doesn't like me. I like him Why?*
> *Why are things like that?*

For what reason in the world? Why?
— Julie, 1978 —

It's not really important why my parents decided to divorce, or my place to tell about the fights and difficulties. Suffice it to say that my parents had personality traits that did not work well together. During the time that my parents were initially deciding to divorce, my older brother, Donnie, went to live with some friends. He did not want to watch our parents break apart, or listen to their arguments. Maybe it was harder for him because he was older. I don't blame him for taking care of himself, but that fourteen-year-old-child who is still a part of me does. The situation was just too hard to handle on my own.

When my parents told me they were going to get divorced, I didn't know what to expect. I was just overwhelmed by the word. No one told me the rules — that I couldn't talk to one about the other. That I could never invite both to the same horse show or school play (at least not in the beginning). That my father would move away, and two days a week would replace growing up with him.

Divorce changes children's relationships with their parents. My mother and I became partners. We went to horse shows, worked the horses, and lived alone, together. My father and I became strangers. Several months after the divorce was final, I began to spend weekends with him. To have my father pick me up at the house was a wrenching experience. More difficult, still, was the realization that I had to watch everything that I said. If I spoke about my mother, my father's face would fall into shadow. He would talk to me about all the things he'd done wrong or what he wished he'd done differently. After weekend trips I would return home and place those days on a dusty shelf in the back of my mind. I could never share with my mother what my father and I had done, because she would become upset or angry. Suddenly I was no longer a child but instead was taking care of my parents.

Sometimes I wonder what kind of person I would have been if my parents had stayed together. Would I have been so obsessed about becoming a jockey? Was I trying to escape the emotional turmoil of my home and the overwhelming frustration of school? Probably some of both, but regardless, my parents' divorce cemented my aspiration to become a jockey.

Eventually, I attained my dream, but it took until the age of thirty to discover the root of my frustration with school. At thirty I discovered I have a learning disorder. All those years of my life spent frustrated with school and with the feelings of inadequacy that they instilled in me were now explained. I could finally understand the little blond child inside me — the one who suppressed the painful memories and whom I can seem to recall only through half-filled diaries and scraps of paper lined with poems.

Miss Hudson's Class
Oh this class is such
a bore. I wish I could
get up and walk out the door.
It's about as exciting as watching
a mouse eat cheese,
or water freeze.
— Julie, 1979 —

Numbers, letters, words. Throughout my school career, I reversed, flip-flopped, and stacked them in an improbable and inexplicable manner. No one ever said the word "dyslexia." I never heard the term "dyscalculia," or the explanation of why sitting still in a seat for more than an hour made me feel sick to my stomach from "Attention Deficit Disorder." Approximately 20 percent of all children have some type of learning disorder — that's five children out of twenty-five in every classroom. I wish I'd known that when I was memorizing the answers to math problems so that when I was called to the blackboard I wouldn't look stupid. Or when teachers would tell me I was a horrible speller, or a slow learner, or a problem student.

Dyslexia is defined in the dictionary as "a disturbance of the ability to read." Dyscalculia is a disturbance in the ability to calculate. It's a real double whammy, because even when I knew how to add, subtract, multiply, and divide, I saw most of my numbers in reverse order. Needless to say, I didn't get many A's in math class. My dyslexia is apparent in my poetry, and while the perfectionist in me wants to rewrite my poems, I think it's important that they remain intact. After all, they represent who I was and a part of the reason for who I am. As for ADD (Attention Deficit Disorder), it refers to general classroom behavior, and indicates a disorder whereby a child does not progress in a satisfactory manner, has difficulty paying attention, and is easily distracted. Sorry, Miss Shilling — I couldn't help myself.

I hated high school. My mother remembers all the school plays I was in and the covers of the playbooks I designed. She remembers me spending time with my best friends, Tracey and

Lori, and watching me walk, trot, and canter Filly or Ralphy, an Arabian horse my mother purchased for me several years after I showed my potential on Filly, as I stood on their backs or did somersaults off their rumps. I remember some of those times, but mostly I recall how frustrated I was because I couldn't seem to learn. At the same time, I was experiencing the particular pain that comes with wondering why everyone was growing up but me. I didn't know in tenth grade that I would never top four feet ten inches; I only knew that I was not growing at the same pace as the other kids in my class. I'm happy about that fact today — I couldn't be a successful jockey if I were tall — but back then, when I wanted attention from boys and to be asked out on dates, it was painful.

Here I sit all alone
thinking how every
thing has grown
even my favorite spot in
the woods has grown
But why can't we stay small
Instead of growing tall
we have to give up things we like
like coloring in a book and
playing in the mud.
I like being a kid but every
good thing comes to an end
so I'd better end this poem
for I'm growing up
I think?
— Julie, 1979 —

The black-and-white photos that my father took of me during my junior high and high school years show a teenager who looks like she is still ten years old — bare feet, blue-jean shorts, T-shirt, and wispy blond hair usually in my eyes. I can remember my father taking pictures of me on my horse, in my tree, and hand-in-hand with my best friends. But the memories of how I felt are cloudy, and at times my poetry is the only remnant of my feelings and emotions that I can touch.

We sit together talk funny, nasty and sometimes
just about the weather . . .
But sometimes I don't feel like I belong
I just don't do the right things say the right
lines . . .
I get put out all too many times
they call I come. When will this school
life be done . . .
They talk about their loves gone and loves
to be. Sometimes they even tell me . . .
I like to be around them they say
I'm funny. I make them laugh but I
just don't feel they play my song
I'm just wanting to be me
and wanting to belong
— Julie, 1979 —

I'm not saying that just because of school, my parents' divorce, or my divided nature about wanting to both grow physically yet still remain a child (with a child's set of responsibilities and lifestyle) I decided to become a jockey. It's not a decision I made because of one thing, but because of what's deep inside me.

In 1978 I watched Steve Cauthen on television as he won the Kentucky Derby aboard a horse named Affirmed. Affirmed was a magnificent horse, whose stride just blew me away, and Steve Cauthen was flawless. I immediately wanted to be a jockey. I went to the bookstore and found a book about Cauthen called *The Kid* by Pete Axthelm. He was just what everybody on television had made him out to be — a kid who rode his butt off, never made mistakes, and was perfect on racehorses. More than that, when he got off, he was a wonderful gentleman, an all-American athlete. I had made my decision. The baseball cards that littered my walls were replaced with photos of Angel Cordero and Jorge Velasquez. At night I dreamed of riding with those legends. By day I plotted ways to achieve my goal.

When I talked with my mother about my dream, she reminded me of 1975, when I was eleven years old and had watched Ruffian break down in a match race with Foolish Pleasure. "What do you mean they're going to kill her!" I had screamed at my mom. I was incredibly upset. All Ruffian had was a broken leg, and in my life horses just didn't die. Cats died, dogs died, all the farm animals died, but other than Ibn, horses were immortal. Later I found out that the vets had done everything possible to save the horse, but eventually had to put her down. At the time, I had some negative thoughts about racing — I couldn't understand how anyone could put a horse to sleep — and never even considered being a jockey. I explained to my mother that I had been a child then. But it wasn't until Chuck Grant took me seriously that my mom gave my decision serious thought.

My mother didn't start riding horses until she was in high school. It had been her dream as a child to be an equestrienne someday. She grew up in Chicago, though, and there was little opportunity to own a horse in the city. Still, she held on to her dream and when her family moved to the suburbs she began to ride. Although her career began late compared to my own, mom quickly developed impressive skills and had an intuitive level of communication with horses. Not only did my mother teach me how to ride and how to build on my intuition with animals, but also it was her desire to constantly improve her own riding that led to my first steps in becoming a jockey.

In the winter of 1979 my mother arranged for renowned dressage instructor Chuck Grant to hold a clinic in our town. My mother and I both took the clinic, and, being the crowd pleaser that I am, I waited until everyone was taking a break and then cantered around the arena standing on my Arabian stallion Ralphy's back. Mr. Grant was properly impressed, and my mother and I were invited to go to lunch with him and his assistant. When everyone was seated, I turned to Mr. Grant and told him that I wanted to be a jockey. My mother just smiled and made some pat-on-the-head type of comment, but Chuck Grant took me seriously. He explained to my mom that a lot of women were becoming involved on the backside of the racetrack (working for trainers in the stable area, galloping and exercising racehorses) and that there were even a few girl jockeys. If Julie is really interested, he said, get some track magazines and books. Learn as much as you can about the sport, then go to a track, find a trainer, and get Julie a job as a hot-walker. So that's what we did.

The next day my mother bought the magazine *Turf and Sport* and a book called *The Shoe*, about jockey Bill Shoemaker. I can remember sitting with her on a mattress in the living room — which we had moved downstairs after my father left so we would be near the woodstove and save on our electric bill — and poring over those books. We studied each picture of the Shoe in his book, trading observations about his body position aboard his horses. Together we decided to travel to Churchill Downs for my sophomore year spring break, to secure a summer job for me at the track.

That winter I helped my mother teach riding at a local barn. We worked long hours and saved as much money as we could for the trip. Mom worked nights at a friend's bar and put all her quarter tips in a big glass jar, which we would later use for gas money. And throughout the entire winter, I dreamed of becoming a jockey.

January 4, 1979 Dear Diary, I punched more holes in my stirrup leathers so my stirrups would be higher. Then I put my saddle on our bench and put my boots on and my hard hat and my overalls and red flannel shirt. Maybe I looked kinda silly holding a fly swatter, but I was practicing switching the whip.

January 7, 1979 Dear Diary, today I rode just at a walk cause it was so cold. I did Steve Cauthens style real low with just my toes in, and Lester Piggot's style with my feet all the way in the stirrups and my rear real high. Then I did Shoe's style — balls of my feet in the stirrup and right in the middle of my horse. Our cats got put to sleep today. They all had lucimea — I cried alot.

January 17, 1979 Dear Diary, WHEW! It's cold out — 12 degrees below zero. I didn't have school so we rode the horses to get milk, candy, ciggarets (for mom), Kool Aid. I'm reading a book called The Track — A Day in the life of Belmont Park — it's good.

January 20, 1979 I never knew there was an advanced position in breezing or racing. Now I do cause we got a thoroughbred encyclopedia.

January 24, 1979 I went riding this morning. Rode about 6½ miles I breezed Ralphy about four miles of and on. I might take him in a few Arab races.

January 27, 1979 Didn't have any school today so I rode my horse really let him go today. I haven't had the chance to even get to use my whip yet cause he's giving me all hes got.

February 2, 1979 Didn't have any school today. It was cold to ride — not for me though, I could ride in a blizzard. My mom just left for work. You know I just realized how much she helps me and how nice she is to me. Maybe its just cause I'm growing up. I hope not! I love her . . .

February 19, 1979 Ma's horse (kelly) had her baby, a boy just like I wanted. Too bad he doesn't have wings, I wanted a stallion with wings. I haven't ridden for a long time cause it's so darn cold — it kills me! I can't wait 'til April when we go to Churchill Downs.

February 21, 1979 I'm in the process of reading a book called *The Lady is A Jock*. Its about woman jockeys — it's wild. I can't even go to sleep. When I do I have dreams that wake me up (about racing). I'm sleeping with my whip now.

February 24, 1979 Boy do I feel lousy today. The boy that I'm going with (Curt) doesn't think I like him no more. But I do but he doesn't believe me. He says most girls when they are going with someone dream about them. I keep having a dream about a horse race in slow motion, over and over again. Every time I watch the race, I get to pick out what I did wrong.

February 28, 1979 Rode Ralphy at 6:00 this morning. I didn't hit Ralphy today, just let him run. My ears were cold, but I can't put a hat on cause it flattens my curls.

March 2, 1979 Rode Ralph after school. I dropped my whip. I knew I was gonna do it even before I did it. I can't do that in a real race or I could kill someone. If I can't control my horse, he might run into somebody else's and that jockey might be thrown. Jockeys get hurt all the time. I've got to learn.

March 4, 1979 Mom told our vet, Doc Shob, that I was gonna be a jockey. He told her to go home and hit me on the head. It's not so bad being a jockey, he said, its the shit that goes along with it. Mom and I haven't been getting a long to well.

I just don't know why. If only she wouldn't keep saying I do every thing for you (she does, but I wish she wouldn't say it all the time).

On the night of April 6th, my mother, our Great Dane, Arrow, and I drove to Churchill Downs. I was so excited that I couldn't sleep. But I was also nervous. We had given ourselves three days to find jobs once we got to the racetrack. There was no other way that we could afford to stay in Kentucky for my entire school vacation. Neither of us had ever worked at a racetrack, and we weren't sure what to expect.

My mother quickly found a job as a hot-walker. It was her responsibility to put a halter on the horse after he was exercised, while the groom placed a blanket over the horse. Then she had to walk him into the large rectangular areas between shed rows, remove the blanket, and hold him while he got his bath. After the bath, she walked the horse for ten minutes, then she allowed him to drink water in small sips (to avoid bellyaches). Finally she walked him until he was completely dry before putting him back in his stall. Then it was time for the next horse.

I watched my mother work for a bit before heading down the shed row to find my own job walking hots. It was more difficult for me. I was a scrawny, tiny little girl, and there weren't many trainers who thought I was qualified to be a hot-walker. At the end of the day, my mother came searching for her daughter. She couldn't find me. She went back to the car and began to drive between the shed rows. Finally, she spied me at Barn 38, and I ran toward her and told her she couldn't come into the barn. "Mom, don't come in here right now, I'm talking to the

trainer about working here as a hot-walker again tomorrow."
My mother returned to the car, and I stayed talking with Clarence and Donna Picou, a young trainer and his wife whose
horses were housed in that barn. They agreed to hire me again
the next day. I skipped to the car.

That evening, Mom and I sat on the pull-out bed in our van
talking and soaking our blistered feet. No one had told us that
you don't wear cowboy boots when you're walking hots. We
had both been educated by the 4-H club, which strongly advises wearing boots around horses at all times so your feet can't
get crushed. Of course, I usually walked barefoot around our
barn, but on that day, I had pulled on a pair of boots to look
my best for the trainers. What a mistake!

Several days later, my mother accepted a job transporting
some racehorses to another track. She assumed that she
would be gone for the afternoon but would return in time to
meet at the van at the end of the day. Mom didn't realize that
there were really six horses being transported, and one was
running the last race. She didn't return until after dark, and
Clarence and Donna took me home to their house for
dinner. It was the best thing that ever happened to me. That
night I explained to Clarence and Donna that I wanted to
spend the summer at Churchill Downs and to become a
jockey eventually. A few days later, they offered me a summer
job. Then it was time for Mom and me to return home.
Spring break was over, and I had to finish my school year
before I could return to Kentucky.

June 7, 1979 Dear Diary, I'm going to Kentucky tomorrow.
To excited, that's all I can write.

*   *   *

The night before my mother drove me back to Churchill
Downs to spend the summer working for Clarence, we saddled
our horses and went for a ride. It was past midnight and the
moon was almost full, shining silver on the road as we cantered
along. We sang the song "Don't Fence Me In" at the top of our
voices, and the neighborhood dogs howled. It was not the last
time we would ride together, but it was the last ride we took as
mother and child.

– 6 –

SUMMER AT THE DOWNS

THE SUMMER I spent at Churchill Downs was an introduction not only to the racetrack but also to adult relationships, the intensity of my own desires, and a type of loneliness I had never before experienced.

Dear Mom,

Boy do I miss you. I miss you a whole lot I feel like crying all the time. I miss you so much, but as they say in France SA,LA,VE (that's life). You used to say just wait till you grow up and move away you'll know how bad you treated your mom (I'm sorry and you know what? I LOVE YOU and miss you to all heck). — Julie

In June of 1979, I was sixteen years old — too young to work legally at the racetrack in Kentucky. My mother altered my birth certificate, taping the word April over July, and photocopied the original. Copy in hand, we drove to Churchill

Downs. Years later, my mother told me how difficult it had been for her to leave me with Clarence and Donna Picou — relative strangers in a place that wasn't home. But at the time, I just gave my mom a quick hug and headed to the barn. Halfway home, she decided to turn around and pick me up. The only thing that stopped her was the understanding that I'd never go back with her.

There is no such thing as a bucket of steam. A saddle stretcher does not exist, and forget the key to the quarter pole. But in my first week of work at Churchill Downs, I attempted to get them all. The steam proved immediately impossible, but the saddle stretcher seemed real enough. I was sent from Barn 38 to Barn 30 to get the stretcher. Once there, I was told the stretcher was in barn 4. However, after arriving at 4, I was told it had been lent to Barn 16. . . . After a few hours of running from shed row to shed row, someone eventually let me in on the joke. It didn't seem very funny then, but I quickly initiated the next greenhorn I could find.

For fifty dollars a week, I worked for Clarence as a hot-walker. One of my main responsibilities was to bathe the horses after a workout. Since I was so tiny, I had to stand straddling the rim of a five-gallon bucket, with the water right to the top, in order to reach both the water and the horse's back. Some-times the system backfired, and the horse would push me, and I'd lose my balance and topple butt down into the soapy bucket. I remember how frustrated I would get, spending every day answering to the order, "Hot-walker, come here." My feet were always wet, and when I'd raise my arm to wash a horse, all the dirty brown water would dribble down to my armpit. But I never got angry or gave up, because I knew that I had a lot to learn, and I knew that there was no better place than the Downs.

In the beginning I had no friends. When my work was done at the track, I had nothing to do. There was a graveyard near the Picous' home, and I spent much of my spare time there, surrounded by crumbling slate and the thick carpet of yellow-green ivy and weeds that blanketed much of the engravings on the headstones. Leaning against the crooked stones, I wrote letters to my mother, drew pictures, and fantasized about who the dead had been. Sometimes I'd trace their names with my fingertips, wondering if they, too, had felt solemn and alone at sixteen.

Dear Mom,

I'm just laying here in bed wishing I was at home with you. I feel so stuffy here — Clarence and Donna won't even let me chew on a weed. They say get that out of your mouth! God, I'm gonna be so stuffy and sour when I get home — oh mom I dont want to be like that. I feel so cramped and useless being so tight and clean. They don't even joke and laugh. I try but they just don't, and I try being a little fun around Donna but she makes me feel like a little twit. — love, Julie

My mother tells a story of how I used to do cartwheels over our horses when they were held down by a running W (a type of harness used to train them from bad habits). I'd plant my hands on either side of their neck and twirl over their head, eyeball to eyeball, while they whinnied. Three weeks after I arrived at Churchill Downs, Clarence made me a groom in his barn. He had noticed how comfortable I was with the high spirited horses, how even when they were quiet, I'd try to do something to make them jump around. After I became a groom, my spirits lifted, and while I still wanted to ride, I was content learning how to wrap a horse's legs for support during and after working out, to blow dirt out of a horse's eyes that had kicked up from the track during racing, to respirate them with herbs to avoid lower respiratory diseases like allergies and infectious bronchitis, and all the other techniques that go into caring for racehorses. If I could have stayed at the barn every night, I would have been completely happy. But every night I returned to my room in the Picous' house. It was a nice enough room, but it wasn't home.

Oh mom,

it must be 2:30 or 3:00 in the morning. I want to call you again but I know some one would get up and say what are you doing? I'd say talking to my mom, they'd say oh no you can't do that hang up your gonna wake someone up. Right now I feel so awful, I can't think of anything happy but you right now. I wish I was home, I would hug you and I wouldn't be sad any more. Oh mom I feel so terrible. Mom, its hard, I can't understand some things different about Clarence and Donna — they are not like people in Michigan. They show there love different and its very hard to accept. I'm use to the real way of someone showing there love, your way, my way.

I spoke to dad about how we decided I could stay working at the Downs in the Fall, and he says that if I want to stay in Kentucky, I have to find a way to go to school or he will cut off your child support.

Mom I can't sleep all I can think of is bad things. Some times Clarences breath smells like liquor and I wonder if its just gum. I want to be home so bad so that we can be together. I feel so alone, everyone is nice and I think they love me but it stops at a certain point. — Love, Julie

It is not fair to write intimate details about Clarence and Donna Picou's relationship. It is enough to say that they worked constantly together, and having a stranger live with them while they dealt with the difficulties of married life was not ideal. At the same time, although the environment was an uncomfortable one, Clarence sensed my unhappiness, and went out of his way to get me on his horses. For that, I will always be grateful.

Every evening Clarence and I walked the length of the barn. We checked the horses' legs, made sure they were watered and well fed, and talked about my desire to become a jockey. Clarence had been a star apprentice jockey before deciding that he wanted to become a trainer, and he would explain things like how to tie the knot in my reins to adjust their length by wrapping them twice where the buckle that connects the rein is, and how to quickly wrap my stirrup leathers around my stirrup in order to make them short enough for me to ride. "But when can I ride?" I'd always ask with a grin.

Late at night I'd sit in my room rifling through the box where Clarence kept all his apprentice jockey memorabilia. There were pictures and articles, and I remember how cool I thought it was that he had hung on to all those things, and how impressed I was by how famous he had been. That's going to be me someday, I'd think. The idea that I wouldn't be a successful jockey, or that I might just be a mediocre jockey, never crossed my mind. Maybe being young, and naive, I was incapable of thinking of failure. Even after witnessing some negative aspects of being a jockey, such as eating disorders and drug abuse, I was not discouraged.

*　　*　　*

Red was a jockey who rode some of Clarence's horses. He was very tall, and was constantly on a diet to make his weight requirement. He also took Lasix, a medicine that prevents a respiratory disorder in horses called EIPH, "exercise-induced pulmonary hemorrhage" (bleeding from the lungs caused when small capillaries around the lungs' air sacs rupture), and keeps humans from retaining water. Red also spent a lot of time in the sweat box, a sauna for jockeys that helps reduce water weight. Red ended up with an inflammation of his liver caused by toxic agents. He had poisoned his own body.

That summer there were other jockeys that were rumored to have bulimia, and it was said that there was a "heaving bowl" (to vomit in before weigh-in) in the jocks' room. How much truth there was to those rumors, I don't know. But to paint a picture of all jockeys as psycho pill-takers with eating disorders would be wrong.

Jockeys are incredible athletes, and they couldn't compete all year long if they were malnourished. They respect their bodies, regardless of whether they have to take Lasix or go into the sweat box once in a while. It's impossible for a human being to stay on a strict diet 365 days a year, a diet where they are not allowed to gain even one pound. Just imagine having one full glass of wine and eating five bites of dinner as opposed to one or two, and knowing that because of that, you're going to gain several pounds. It's almost as if the sport itself forces jockeys to use Lasix or the box for the infrequent times when they decide to eat a complete meal. That summer at Churchill Downs, Clarence assured me that because of my height and build I'd never have a weight problem. He was right, but regardless, Red's illness and all the rumors taught me a valuable lesson.

*　　*　　*

When it finally happened, it was like a dream. I could hear Clarence's voice echoing in the background, but the thundering of hooves and the wild cheers of the Kentucky Derby crowd drowned out his cautions of "Don't let him get away now, pull, pull," until they were almost a whisper. I was galloping my first racehorse down the stretch at Churchill Downs, Clarence riding the lead pony by my side. I set my face in a stony grimace, determined not to let him see how hard I was working to keep the horse in control. It took two days before the high wore off. After that, Clarence began to let me gallop horses every day.

Dear mom,

I breezed two horses this morning. Clarence complemented me and I never thought nothing of it. Ok, so I did good. I mean I felt wonderful inside, but I didn't say anything. After he told me how good I did, he kept saying over and over don't get cocky, you know tomorrow you could be cleaning a stall. Jeeze, I know that — Julie

Dearest Mom,

I have a very good friend named Robin. She's 32 years old and she owned jumpers and has shown all her life. She is working some for Clarence. She's super and she loves me and I love her and it helps me so much just to be around her. She has real horse sense she just thinks like you about life and people. I told her how great she was, how she's uplifted my spirits and made me feel like my self, my home self. I even talked to her about Donna, and she made me feel much better. I talked to her just like I do you and she answered just like you. I've never known two people so alike.

We drove to Latonia last night and watched the races. It was so beautiful it made me want to ride so much! On the way home, Donna and Robin rode in the front together, and the first thing Donna said was, did Julie talk your ear off? Robin said no (ha!).

Mom we passed so many beautiful farms — oohh beautiful — they are the kind I'm gonna buy you and your gonna instruct. Well I'm tired and Im gonna go to sleep. Please dear mother send me pictures, some winter close, my pimple stuff from doctor Wilson, my pillow and my red coat and you! Love, Julie

Clarence gave me the responsibility of riding the lead pony to take his horses to the paddock before races. Every barn has lead ponies, horses or ponies used to guide racehorses through their morning exercises and teach them to walk when it's necessary. They are a calming force and provide racehorses with a sense of security and a model for appropriate behavior. Each day after I returned with his pony, Clarence would send me down the' road with instructions to "Cool him down, don't ride him hard." I'd smile and say, Yes, yes, Clarence, and as soon as we were out of sight of the barn, I'd hike up my stirrups, get into my best jockey position, and tear off down the road. In my mind I'd be racing along the stretch in a fierce battle with Affirmed and Alydar, pulling out in front at the last moment to win by a nose. It would take me an hour to cool the lead pony down enough to bring him back to the barn. When I'd return, Clarence would check for sweat marks and say, "Did you ride that horse hard?" I'd look up at him innocently and say, "Of course not."

Dear mom,

I went to the sale at Keenland track and I met Buddy Delp

*(trainer) and other important people. I've been galloping about 4
horses every morning, and today one of the horses I galloped, Tonto,
was second in the big stakes race Wow!*

*On the drive home from the race, Donna told me that when we
got home I had to pick up the apples in the yard. I said in a joking
way "nope, I'm not gonna," and boy did she get upset. Teenagers
shouldn't joke with older people. I think Donna would be a terrible
mom, once her kid came out of the shell she'd probably put it back in.*

*Things are getting worse at home I'm not sure I should stay here
to go to school in the Fall . . . Any way, sometimes I feel like I'm
wasting time with my life instead of spending it with my mom and
my friends and my horse. If I was home I could help you with lessons
and we could go on trail rides together. I hope things are a little better
than they were before I left. Oh Momie, I love you! Julie*

In August of 1979, my mother got sick and had to have a
hysterectomy. She spent several weeks recuperating, and during that time it became clear that I needed to move out of the
Picous' house. I flew back to Michigan when my mother was
well enough to have me home. When I got off the airplane, I
raced to the car and kissed our Michigan tags. My mom
couldn't get over how solid and strong I'd become over the
summer. And I couldn't get over how much I'd missed her and
how happy I was to be enfolded in her hug. The only drawback
to my return? I was just in time to begin my junior year of high
school.

- 7 -

HIGH SCHOOL DAZE

WHEN I RETURNED to school in the fall of 1979 nothing had changed. Nothing, except that everyone else continued to grow and I continued to rush home after school and ride the horses, mush my Great Dane, and wrap my spirit in the blustery winter winds that frosted my eyelashes and reddened my nose. The world was changing around me. Lori was in love, and the other girls in my class were focused on clothes, makeup, and dating. But my personal world remained the same. At least on the outside. Inside I was also changing. The problem was that no one could see those changes, and I could only share with Tracey, Lori, and my animals my unhappiness about not fitting in and my growing desire to leave Eau Claire and become a professional jockey.

I could still smell the racetrack and feel the vibrations in the soles of my feet as a pack of horses tore down the stretch. But

I was in Michigan, going to classes that filled me with mounting frustration, and living in a house that had lost its family.

> *In the quiet of the evening*
> *when the dark was falling fast*
> *I sat in my room and thought of the*
> *things I had done in the years gone past.*
> *But my thoughts were disturbed by the knowledge*
> *that some where along the way*
> *I had failed in my half-hearted efforts*
> *to live virtuously every day.*
> *So agervated did my mind wander*
> *for I knew I had miss understood*
> *the importance of that extra some thing*
> *that separates evil from good . . .*
> — *Julie* —

Lori and I fell back into our habit of skipping some classes and occasionally smoking pot. My mother didn't know how to stop me. She'd never tried to control me before, and when the time came that I needed direction, she didn't know how to give it.

> *As my friends and I play*
> *in our own way.*
> *Having just as much fun as any other day.*
> *My body sitting by the door my mind starts to*
> *wander as its done so many times before.*
> *No longer sitting in a car with smoke*
> *filling the air.*

Now in a land where everything is peaceful and fair.
The children play in their own special way.
Having more fun than the other day.
My mind soars and soars
then returns to my body
and I'm sitting by the door.
I fight with myself
I say I don't want to do this anymore.
Confused, I'll just do it again,
when will we ever win?
Just another sin.
— Julie, 1979 —

My mom did the only thing she felt might help. When my junior year ended, she sent me to live with her girlfriend Pat Sachen, whose husband raced quarter horses. The Sachens lived an hour from our home, right next to a Michigan racetrack. Pat's husband agreed not only to let me live with his family for the entire summer but also to allow me to race some of his horses. My mom was thrilled. She believed that if my spirit was involved in the excitement of racing, perhaps trouble wouldn't follow me.

I spent the summer of 1980 racing in Michigan, Ohio, and Illinois. The circuit of fair tracks I raced had non–pari-mutuel wagering, which means no betting, just racing for the purse. There were quarter horses, Appaloosas, and Arabians, and I rode about sixty races. That summer I learned how to switch sticks (move the whip quickly from one hand to the other). Previously when I was riding, instead of switching I would hold the whip in my right hand and reach over to hit the horse on the left side. After the race, one of the jockeys told me that wasn't the correct way to whip. We walked to a barn and sat atop big yellow bales of straw as he explained the right way, and showed me how to practice. That meant a lot to me, because being able to switch the whip quickly is a skill that's held in very high regard by jockeys.

"Don't worry about being trampled by the other horses when you fall off, 'cause you'll be so far behind the pack that you won't get hurt." That's what Pat Sachen's husband said to me on July 4, 1980, before my first 440-yard quarter horse race. I placed second by a whisker. Soon after, I began to win, and other trainers started letting me ride their horses. When I'd ride onto the fair track in Michigan, the announcer would say, "There's Julie Krone, one of the best little jockeys, male or female, we've had at the fair in ages." I was a big fish in a small pond, but I was still swimming in dangerous waters. Perhaps that's because I've always been the type of person that has to learn from her mistakes. Some people can be told don't do that, it's wrong, or, it will end up hurting you. Others have to hurt themselves, and learn from that experience. While it would take several years and not a few heartbreaks, I would eventually learn. For me the time went by quickly — I was a steaming locomotive, barreling down the tracks, at times derailing, but always learning how to correct my errors. But for my mother, those years seemed to stretch toward infinity.

> *Mother, you say that I'm a sneaky*
> *kid and that maybe you should*
> *have when I was a baby*
> *drowned me in a lake*

you've never baked me a cake.
Then why do I love you
like I do — this I wondered
as I grew.
Your the one who bought
my first horse. You taught me
how to ride and be the best
(of course).
I know that you love me dearly
you tell me more than once
yearly.
I can't be perfect for I'm
only seventeen you see but then
if I was whose fault would it be?
— Julie, 1979 —

What I remember most about both my junior and senior years of high school is that I don't remember much. My memories are hazy, perhaps because of my unhappiness. I returned from the racetrack to begin my senior year of high school. It was uneventful until December, 1980, when my mother, having seen by my success over the summer on the fair tracks that I had the potential to become a successful jockey, decided to let me drop out of school and go live with my grandparents in Tampa, Florida, to pursue my dream.

My father was not happy with the decision. He believed I was giving up on school. His perspective was one of a junior high school teacher who had seen too many kids drop out. I felt I was sacrificing school in order to become a jockey. Being torn between parents and their idea of what's wrong and right is an extremely agonizing position. But it taught me how to manipulate two fiercely opposed forces, a skill that would later become invaluable for my success as a jockey. I dropped out of school.

My mother wasn't upset. She had hated school, too. It was the part about sending her daughter to live thousands of miles away that got to her. My mom believed that I had the experience and raw talent that I needed to become a jockey, but she was still sending her daughter into unknown territory.

Money was tight, and in order to get me from Michigan to Tampa, my mom had to ask her aunt Inez and uncle Bud (my grandfather's sister and her husband) to drive me down to her parents' home. My mother did not have enough money to travel with me.

Armed with the win photos that my father had taken the previous summer — absolutely beautiful photos, which showed not only my raw talent as I tore down the stretch on the back of a racehorse, but also my father's artistry and magic behind the camera — and my boots, hat, crop, and small suitcase of clothes, I hugged my mother good-bye and hopped into my relatives' van. My mother looked so alone as we drove away. Alone, and smaller than her five-foot-one-inch height.

It took Mom less than an hour to have second thoughts. What am I doing, letting Julie go down to Tampa alone, she muttered to herself all the way home. How in the world was her daughter going to get a job at the racetrack — who would watch out for her? Mom drove straight to the bus station, bought a ticket to Tampa, and settled in her seat for the long ride. We arrived at my grandparents' home the same afternoon.

The next morning, my mother and I, not having passes, climbed over the back fence of Tampa Bay Downs. A wire fence and the absence of passes wasn't going to stop us from reaching our goal. We were two tiny women with an enormous dream. We strode down the dirt road toward the shed rows where the trainers, riders, and horses were beginning their day. I remember I was carrying a crop and wearing leather boots and the blue-and-white riding hat my mother had purchased for me the previous summer. I was ready to ride. Less than a hundred yards down the road, a white Cadillac pulled over and a young woman asked us where we were going. (She told us later that at first she had thought we were two young kids.) I immediately told her that I had come to Tampa to become a jockey. "Hop in. Let's go see my trainer," she said.

The woman's name was Denise, and she was an assistant trainer. By the time we got to the barn I'd shown her all my win pictures and told her I planned to become a professional jockey. Denise explained to me that her boyfriend (later her husband), Jerry Pace, was a trainer, and that every year he helped one little kid become an apprentice jockey. When we walked over to Jerry, Denise said, "Jerry, this girl wants to be a jockey. She'd like to get on some of your horses." He turned to look at me, jingling the change in his pocket and fixing me with a wide grin. "So, little girl, you wanna be a jockey, huh?" "No sir," I replied, "I'm *gonna* be a jockey." Jerry laughed, then took me to his barn to ride one of his horses. She was a little black filly named Tiny Star, and she would end up being my first mount at Tampa. I galloped her while Jerry watched. He put me on several more horses, and when I was finished, he told me to come back the next day. I couldn't stop jumping up and down with excitement when I left Jerry's barn.

The next day I rode a few more horses, and the following day, Jerry took me to the Tampa Bay Downs office and got me an exercise license. On the fourth day, he put me in the gate and let me start some horses. Learning how to start racehorses is extremely important for a jockey, not only because of the skill involved, but also because of the danger. A horse can become frightened or nervous in the starting gate and seriously injure a rider, other riders, or the gate crew. A jockey has to know how to control her horse from the moment she approaches the gate to the split second she bursts out of it. I was a quick study, and by my fifth day at Tampa, Jerry called the stewards and had them watch me in the gate to qualify me for my jockey's license. Only five days, and I had a job, an exercise and jockey's license, and a trainer who believed in me. At the end of the fifth day, my mother returned home, leaving me to live with her parents. She felt certain that I was on my way.

Jerry Pace used to walk around the barn whistling a happy song. He taught me the words to the tune, and to this day, when I'm feeling down I find myself singing that song. It was a lucky thing for me that Jerry's personality was so kind and forgiving, and that his sense of humor was as bright as his smile — I knew a lot about horses, but not much about the racetrack.

"How the hell am I supposed to put you on a racehorse if you don't know where the poles are?" Jerry would half-teasingly yell at me. I only knew the pole distances at the Michigan fair tracks. Tampa's track was a different length. "Go a half mile," Jerry would instruct as I galloped a horse. I'd go three quarters of a mile. "Gallop her a mile and a half." I'd call over, "Where do I start?" "Oy," he'd mutter, running his fingers through his curly hair. Finally Jerry told me to get a map of the track and study it. I had a map at my grandmother's house, and I hung it over my bed and began to memorize it. Unfortunately, the map I had was for a mile and an eighth track in Michigan. Tampa was a mile track.

Jerry never gave up on me. "That girl's going to be a very famous jockey someday, and her picture is going to be on the front of magazines," he'd tell fellow trainers and owners. I can't stress how much Jerry did for me that winter. A basketball player can spend hours, days, years practicing his jump shot, and a football player can practice kicking seventy field goals a day, but it's impossible for a jockey to practice unless someone gives her a chance. Jerry Pace gave me that chance, and by allowing me to get on his horses as an apprentice jockey, he greatly affected my career. But he didn't stop there.

I rode my first race, for Jerry, at Tampa on January 30, 1981, on Tiny Star. She finished second, and at the time I felt that we could have won if I'd been allowed to carry a whip. Tiny Star tended to drift out on the turn, and to keep her in I needed a stick. For their first three races, apprentice jockeys can't carry whips, because they might get too excited and hit their horse in a way that would make him duck in or out and impede another horse. Basically, racetracks are afraid that apprentices might hurt someone else. I was very offended by the rule at that time, because I could already switch sticks and knew I wasn't a danger to the other riders. Regardless, Jerry and Denise were happy that their horse had come in second, and I was excited to have done well in my first race — so excited and exhausted, in fact, that when I hopped off Tiny Star my legs crumpled and I fell right on my behind.

"If it was up to me, darlin', I'd let you ride all my horses," Jerry would say on the days that none of his owners would let a girl apprentice jockey ride their horses. No matter what he said, I always felt bad. Jerry understood, and began to drum up business for me outside his own barn. "Come on , you've got to put this little girl on one of your horses," Jerry would say to trainers. Finally Les St. Leon agreed to watch me ride his horse, Lord Farkle, who everyone knew was just getting ready to win. He was a gigantic chestnut, over seventeen hands, with four white socks and a big white blaze. I got on and breezed him (raced at a moderate speed for a short distance), but broke off from the wrong pole (markers at different points around the track that measure the distance to the finish). "How am I supposed to put you on your first racehorse that wins if you don't even know where the poles are?" Les said with a laugh as I rode up to him.

Les St. Leon let me ride Lord Farkle anyway. And on February 12, 1981, I won my first race as an apprentice jockey at Tampa Bay Downs. As we thundered down the stretch I kept thinking, When are all the horses going to pass me? And as I hit the wire, I had to look over my shoulder and double check that I was in front, that no one had slipped by. No one had, and I rode to the winner's circle.

When an apprentice jockey wins her first race, it's called "breaking her maiden." There is a time-honored tradition connected to that win, involving peanut butter, black shoe polish, baby powder, and shaving cream. When I returned to

the jocks' room after my win, ten jockeys descended on me —
there was no way to escape. They covered me, head to toe, with
their sticky laurels. It happens to everyone, and when an apprentice breaks her maiden, absolutely nothing, not even that
tradition, can wipe the smile off her face.

– 8 –

THE FIRST BIG MOVE

"JULIE SNELLINGS SAYS you should raise your butt, lower your heels. . . ." It was that type of advice I'd hear every time I got off a racehorse at Tampa Bay Downs. Now, I liked getting suggestions from people I know, even if I know them only by reputation, but I had never heard of Julie Snellings. "Who is this Julie Snellings?" I finally asked. Someone told me that Julie worked in the track office, and I went to confront her.

"If you're so good at riding, why don't you get out on the track and ride," I said to the petite brunette sitting behind the desk. Julie Snellings looked up at me and smiled. Then she rolled her wheelchair far enough back so I could see it. "I was a jockey," she explained softly, "but I fell off at Delaware Park and was paralyzed." I didn't know what to say. "Let's talk about your riding," Julie said as she wheeled herself over to me. "Where are you going when the Tampa meet is over?" Where was I going? I had no answer. I hadn't even thought that far ahead. "You should go to Maryland," Julie said. "I'm going to call some people for you."

Julie enlisted the help of Mrs. Donovan, a Tampa trainer's wife who had taken a liking to what she called my "grit and determination." Together they contacted Chick Lang Jr., an agent in Maryland. "We've got a bug rider for you," they told Chick. (Apprentice riders are called bug riders because an asterisk that looks like a bug appears by their name on the program; they become jockeys when they ride a certain number of winners within a specified period of time.) "What's his name?" Chick asked. "Her name is Julie Krone," Mrs. Donovan replied. "Call me back after she has a sex change," Chick said before he hung up the phone. Taking on a new apprentice rider is tough, and taking on a girl apprentice is even tougher.

When I first began to ride, a lot of owners, trainers, and agents just didn't think girl jockeys could be good riders. But one female had blazed a trail for me, proving that women have the tenacity and aggressive nature required for the sport.

In 1969 Patricia Barton won 179 races, more than any female rider had ever won. She was the leading female jockey in the world until 1984 when she took a bad spill. But it wasn't the number of races Barton won that made her so famous or appreciated by the women in the sport. It was the fact that she stuck her foot in the door of a male-dominated sport and refused to take it out. She was boycotted by male jockeys, who, regardless of her credentials, believed that she was incapable of being a jockey. Her trailer (there was no female jockeys' locker room then) was stoned, and she was subjected to the insults of fans, trainers, and owners. But Patti Barton refused to quit.

I'm the next generation, one of the jockeys, in addition to

Patti's own daughter, Donna, who has benefited from her tenacity. When I entered the sport, it was still almost totally male, and there were definite prejudices among agents, trainers, owners, and jockeys, but at least Patti had opened the door a crack. Of course, I was determined to bust it off its hinges. But the first few years were extremely difficult.

It took several more conversations before Chick agreed to become my agent and to allow me to live with his family while I rode. Without the latter offer, I couldn't have afforded to make the move. When the Tampa meet ended, I boarded a plane for Maryland. "Where are your bags?" Chick asked as we stood by the baggage carousel in the Maryland airport. "Right there," I said, pointing to the cardboard boxes dropping onto the conveyor belt. "Boxes?" he said, rolling his eyes. "Yeah. What's wrong with boxes?" I retorted.

We drove in silence until we reached the top of a hill that overlooked a residential subdivision in Chick's town, Timonium. "Wow, look at all those lights. What a big city," I said in amazement. Up until that point the biggest town I'd been in was Tampa, which was so flat that it didn't look like a large city. Chick laughed. Timonium was a very small town. "Oh, no," he said, "what have I gotten myself into."

When we arrived at the Langs' home, I met Jean, Chick's wife, and their four children, Bart, Tiffany, Devon, and Jaime, along with Kenny Black, Chick's bug rider, who was just finishing his apprenticeship. Kenny was a very successful rider, quite a star. He lived at the Langs', too, but was planning to move into his own apartment. I was really in awe of him. The first night I spent at the Langs', Kenny sat down at the kitchen table with me and described the Pimlico racetrack and all the jockeys. He was really savvy, had an incredible memory about each jockey's riding style, and had tremendous intensity about the sport. That night as I lay on the pull-out couch, I thought about how lucky I was to have the opportunity to learn about racing from Kenny, and to be living with a big family.

I couldn't sleep that first night, so I sat in darkness illuminated by silvery moonbeams and leafed through a coffee-table book on racing. There was a big picture of an apprentice jockey who had been the second-leading bug rider in the nation behind Steve Cauthen. His name was Butchie Essman, and he rode for John Forbes's stable. I remember wishing that I would some day get the opportunity to ride for a great trainer like John Forbes. At the bottom of the page there was a small paragraph that read "Butchie Essman is still in a coma after being hit while on a moped in the Bahamas. Essman was visiting the island while recuperating from an ankle injury."

The Langs were more than a big family. They were loving, close, and a lot of fun. Jean Lang is an incredible mother, and one of the female role models whose strength, caring, coolness under pressure, and diligence I try to emulate. She did a fantastic job of raising her children and giving them wonderful values. And even with four children, she always had time to make me feel like a part of the family. There was a set dinnertime at the Langs', something I had had little experience with. My first week with the family I showed up for dinner a half hour late. They were all sitting at the table, waiting. The food was out, but no one had touched a thing. "Julie, we are sitting here waiting for you," Jean said. I never was late for a meal again.

Kenny Black was also a part of that family, but when he moved to California to race, he stopped calling and writing the Langs. The kids and Chick and Jean were very sad about that. Kenny was having his own problems. He had grown too tall and had begun to use cocaine to keep his weight down. He was suspended for drug use several times, and after refusing to attend the track's drug therapy program, he eventually stopped riding in California.

Regardless of his drug problem, I will always value Kenny's impact on my life. I don't know if he ever realized what a hero he was to everyone — me, the Lang kids, other jockeys. He was a genuinely gifted athlete and a wonderful rider, and I'll always be grateful to him for the insights he shared with me about the sport. After we learned about Kenny's difficulties, I promised the Langs that I would never get into trouble with drugs, leave their home, or stop writing them letters.

I broke some of my promises.

Until a trainer knows you and likes you, it's impossible to get on his horses. No one knew me in Maryland, and I went from galloping and riding racehorses every day in Tampa to riding no horses. I was an unknown girl jockey, and no one wanted me. Every morning I'd go to the Pimlico racetrack and talk to trainers like Bud Delp, John Forbes, Scottie Reagan, and King Leatherbury. I was my smartest, cutest, most sincere — for months. "I'd let you ride, but my owner doesn't want you," trainers would say. It wasn't their fault; trainers have to do what their owners want — even if the owner is dead wrong. I'd just smile when I was rejected, and try again the next day.

I rode any long shot that a trainer would put me on. Even

though my horses would finish last, I tried to ride perfectly, make sure all my tack was impeccable, my pants clean, and my track record spotless. In the mornings, if I was fortunate enough to get to gallop a horse, I always tried my very best to give a hundred and ten percent.

Sometimes a hundred and ten percent is enough. At a party for the winner of the Butchie Essman Apprentice Jockey Award (Essman had died from his moped injury), I was approached by Gerald Delp, trainer Bud Delp's son. "My father is going to let you ride a lot of his horses," he said. Bud Delp had won the Kentucky Derby with Spectacular Bid. "Yeah, right," I said to Gerald. "Sure he's going to let me ride." On my first trip to Churchill Downs, I had watched Bud Delp's horse win the Derby from my perch atop Clarence's barn. At the time, I'd dreamed that someday I would ride for Delp. Dreams like that just didn't come true. "I'm serious," Gerald countered. "But we want to keep this in the family, so I'd have to be your agent." "Come on, Gerald, stop teasing me," I pleaded throughout the evening. "I'm going to take back the offer in a minute, and then you'll be sorry," he said. I began to take him seriously. "I have to talk to Chick first," I said.

Chick Lang was family. How could I drop family and take Gerald as my agent? It was a silly thought. More than anything, Chick wanted me to be a success. I spent the next day nervously anticipating our conversation. "Are you kidding!" Chick yelled. "That's a fantastic opportunity! Take it!" So I did, and it was the beginning of something great.

- 9 -

THE DOPE ON DRUGS

WHEN I BEGAN to ride for Bud Delp, I entered a circle of young people who were active with drugs. It doesn't really matter who my new friends were, just that we were all young and stupid. Most of us now realize how lucky we are to have lived through that time in our lives. It is a time that I look back on and wish I could forget. But I recognize that it taught me some very valuable lessons.

"Julie, I've been hearing some bad things about you. You'd better watch out," an older jockey warned in the winter of 1982. I didn't listen. The following week, racetrack personnel searched my car and found a joint in the ashtray. When you enter a racetrack you are under the jurisdiction of the track's officials. They had every right to search my car and to severely reprimand me for my drug use. I was given a sixty-day suspension and ordered to attend a drug abuse program. But that wasn't the worst part.

The worst part had nothing to do with my suspension or the negative publicity I received. It had to do with disappointing Chick, Jean, their children, and all the trainers who had helped me. It was the first time in my life I realized that my actions could seriously reflect on other people. Chick's father, Chick Lang Sr., was the general manager at Pimlico, and because he had cared for me and befriended me, his reputation was smudged by my actions. I was a disappointment to myself and to the people that I loved. That included my mother, who, having seen my drug use firsthand, had told me the previous year not to call her until I had cleaned up my act. I hadn't spoken with her for months, and it was only after I attended the track's drug abuse program that I found the courage to apologize to her.

Mother your daughter is crying
out in the night and cold,
let me in and forgive me, I'll never
be bad any more. I'm oh so
sick and so sorry, please dear
mother, don't scold it's just
your daughter and she wants
you . . . Mother open the door. . . .
— Julie, spring, 1982 —

No one wants to believe that they are an addict. It was only after attending the racetrack's drug abuse program that I realized I was addicted to marijuana. The program only lasted a month, but it affected me for eternity. It made me aware of my personality type and educated me about all the negative results of drug use. I didn't admit that I was addicted to drugs until the end of the program, but by finally saying it I was liberated. Throughout the time I was in the track's drug program I was not allowed to ride racehorses. The absence of horses in my life was devastating. I would drive to Pimlico and stand on the outside of the fence watching the horses race past the three-eighths pole and knowing that this was one fence I couldn't climb. I learned that the tradeoff for doing drugs versus riding wasn't even an option — I had to ride.

Throughout that difficult and emotional time, Chick and Jean never yelled at me. Instead they were totally supportive and helpful. Chick once again acted as my agent and he arranged for me to be drug tested, so that I could be back on the track galloping horses in thirty days instead of sixty. And several trainers took me back into their barn, giving me a second chance to attain my dream. One of those trainers was Steve Brown.

I met Steve Brown, an assistant trainer for John Forbes, in the fall of 1981, months before I was caught with drugs. John had a string of horses in Maryland that were being supervised by Steve, and Steve began to let me ride those horses, although at the time John didn't know that his assistant was using a girl jockey. When he found out, he was incredulous. "J. Krone is a girl?" said Forbes. "I never thought I'd see the day that you'd use a girl rider." Steve explained, "John, this one can actually ride." I continued to ride for John Forbes's stable once I had beaten my drug problem, but I didn't meet Forbes himself until I began to ride in New Jersey at the Meadowlands and Monmouth.

A year after we met, Steve Brown and I began to date. "Do

you want to go to a Washington Capitals game?" he asked me one afternoon. I just stood there like a statue, with my mouth hanging open. Someone actually wanted to do something with me! At the time I had few friends and spent most of my best times in the jockeys' room, riding horses, or going to the movies by myself. There wasn't much time to socialize, and no one to socialize with. When Steve asked me to go to the hockey game, I was genuinely overwhelmed. He was such a figure of strength for me. His advice was always thoughtful, and I trusted his opinion. He also had a wonderful family, and we spent a lot of time visiting them. There was a lot of laughter in our relationship then, even though I was under a great deal of pressure.

In the winter of 1982 I was scheduled to lose my apprenticeship. One year after a "baby jockey," a jockey not yet officially apprenticed, wins her fifth race, her apprenticeship begins. That apprenticeship lasts one year from that date, and during that time the jockey is allowed a smaller weight allowance than the other riders — her horse runs lighter. At the end of that year, the apprentice becomes a journeyman, and the weight allowances no longer work in her favor, because she has earned the right to ride on an equal basis with the other jockeys. There is no longer an advantage for trainers to ride her. Their horses now have to carry additional weight, and when that happens, trainers prefer seasoned jockeys, who have a better chance of riding a winner.

There is a balcony above the tunnel at Pimlico Race Course, where the audience can watch the horses and jockeys ride onto the track. Before I lost my bug, I used to sit up in the stands, sometimes all day, and watch the races. "Am I gonna be okay when I lose my bug?" I'd ask whatever valet or jockey was sitting near me. They always assured me that I was going to do well, but their words didn't help. Today when I ride a big stakes race at Pimlico and see those people I used to ask for reassurance from, they all tease me. "Am I going to be okay?" they joke in a tiny, scared voice. It's nice to look back on a terrifying time in my life and be able to laugh about it.

But make no mistake, it was a frightening time. While Bud Delp and Steve Brown were riding me, I still had a lot of time to worry about my future. "I'm better than most of those riders," I'd complain to Chick. "Why can't we get them to put me on that horse?" Chick would just smile and tell me stories about Kenny Black and how he used to say the same things when he was a bug. At the time I didn't care, I just wanted a guarantee that after I lost my bug I would still ride.

And I did ride. In my first big race day as a journeyman (at Bowie racetrack in Maryland), I won four races. That didn't mean that every trainer wanted to ride me, but enough paid attention that I was kept busy — until I broke my back.

Timing is everything. Breaking my back only weeks after I'd lost my bug was very bad timing, because my reputation as a journeyman (professional rider) and as a drug-free individual was still tenuous. I was working a horse for Steve Brown. She was a nice little chestnut filly, very fast. That day she was wearing polo bandages on her legs, cloth strips that are usually wrapped from the bottom of the ankle up and then fastened with a safety pin where the wrapping began. Unfortunately, my filly's bandages were not fastened at the base of the bandage but at the top, which isn't necessarily bad, but is a little less safe.

The tractors were just finishing harrowing the track as I walked the filly behind the starting gate. She was bored, so I let her play and paw in a mud puddle. When the tractors were done, we moved into the starting gate. My filly's bandages, now wet, began to draw down, and before we left the gate, one of her front bandages had slipped out. When we broke from the gate, the filly's hind legs caught the trailing bandage.

It was as if someone had taken a hook, wrapped it around my horse's front legs, and given it a quick, powerful jerk. I flew over the filly's head like a pebble from a slingshot, and we hit the ground at the same time — her head between my legs. It happened quickly, but I can still remember the feeling of sliding along the dirt, slowing, and then the crushing weight of the horse rolling on top of my body. After that, everything was a blur. I couldn't breathe very well, and I remember squeezing the paramedic's arm so tightly that later someone told me he was bruised for days.

My T-12 vertebra was compressed and chipped. The doctors ordered me to spend three months resting. Three months? I couldn't spend more than twenty minutes sitting still. I lay in the emergency room at the hospital and began to cry, not so much from the pain but from the fear of what a three-month hiatus would do to my riding career. "Hey, that's my sister," I heard from a curtained-off area. Then Donnie was at my side, dressed in a hospital gown. "What're you doing here?" I asked him. After Donnie had left home he had attended an automotive college before choosing to return to the world of horses that we both had grown up in. He had ended up in Maryland as an exercise rider for several trainers. Donnie explained to me that he had been working a horse when the bridle had slipped off, the horse had reared, and its head had hit Donnie right in the cannolis, hard. That almost made me laugh.

Three weeks later I was walking around with a back brace, and a month after my accident I began to ride. In the spring of 1982 I left Maryland and went to the meet at Atlantic City Race Course in McKee City, New Jersey. Every North American racetrack has a set season or meet during the year. Meets vary in length from weeks to months depending on the availability of horses. The Atlantic City meet begins in June and runs through September. In the first race at Atlantic City that I rode for Steve Brown and John Forbes, I dropped my whip and still won by a nose. The rest of the meet was slow for me. Moving from Maryland to New Jersey was like starting all over again. A lot of the trainers didn't know me and chose not to ride me. I had a new agent, Pat Flynn. I'd wanted Chick to represent me, but he was based in Maryland and I needed someone in New Jersey. Every morning we made our rounds, talked to trainers, and tried to get mounts. After the turmoil of the past year, I was content with the horses I got and was happy to spend my days off at the beach hanging out with new, clean friends. Still, we did a good job, because I ended up the leading rider at Atlantic City that year. I would repeat that feat in 1983.

Chris Antley was my number-one buddy in Atlantic City. Chris was from South Carolina. He'd been fishing at a pond near a stable that broke young horses when a trainer who needed extra help spotted him and asked if he'd like some work. Chris began to hot-walk horses, muck stalls, and dream about becoming a jockey. He didn't start riding for a trainer until he was fourteen years old. That year he began galloping horses for Hamilton Smith. I was visiting Hamilton's barn to see if I could get on some of his babies, and I noticed Chris walking hots. He was such an adorable little boy, really sweet, with a cute accent. Over the next few weeks we got to know each other and ended up spending much of our free time together at the beach. I can still see Chris with his tan pants, Docksiders, and the beanie hat that all the jockeys wore to look like Steve Cauthen. In the evenings, after my races were finished, I'd wander over to Hamilton's barn and see Chris sitting atop a bale of hay pretending he was riding a race. I knew even then that he would become a great jockey. But I never guessed that he'd end up passing me at one point in my career.

During the Atlantic City meet, I finally met John Forbes, Steve Brown's boss and one of the most respected trainers in the racing world. John had a horse running at New Jersey's Monmouth Park. All the horse's papers — a horse's foal certificate that identifies him and must be present at every meet — were in Atlantic City, where he had last run. The day of the race John realized that the papers were missing and knew that if he didn't get them he'd have to scratch his horse. "Don't worry," Steve told him, "Julie Krone is at Atlantic City; I'll have her drive the papers over, and then you can finally meet her." Unfortunately, Steve didn't know my sense of direction.

While the owner of the horse, his wife and daughter, stood in the paddock waiting with Forbes, the first call came over the loudspeakers. They couldn't send the horse out to the track, because they still didn't have his papers. The horse was ready, saddle on, jockey poised to jump on his back, but no Julie Krone, and no papers. As the horses moved out, John was forced to scratch his entry. Now he *really* wanted to meet me.

To drive from Atlantic City to Monmouth you take the

Garden State Parkway and exit at 105. It's a straight line. When I finally arrived at Monmouth, John was pretty angry. "Where the hell have you been!" he yelled. "I got lost," I explained. John didn't hold a grudge for long, and as he remembers it, he began to like me that first day. Or at least he decided that I wasn't run-of-the-mill. And I decided that I wanted to ride for John Forbes.

When the late September meet began at the Meadowlands in New Jersey, I stuck to John Forbes's barn like glue. At that point I was looking for a home. A young jockey's goal is to ride for a reputable stable that has great trainers and high caliber horses. Working for Forbes would not only provide me with the opportunity to ride more winners, but his expertise would help me continue my education as a jockey. Even if Steve hadn't worked for John, I still would have come knocking on his door. He took me in, and I became family.

What I learned from John Forbes can be divided into two categories, personal and professional. I'll start with the latter. When I began riding for John, I was still learning how to communicate with trainers. A jockey is a translator from horse to trainer. When I gallop a horse, I have to talk to him with my body, my hands, and my voice and in turn tell the trainer just what his horse is thinking and doing. I knew how to communicate with horses, but John taught me how to communicate with him. At the same time, he calmed me down a bit. I was still pretty flighty — a mixture of talent and screw-up. John taught me to always be where I was supposed to be, on time, and a professional.

Years ago there was a horse that was famous for being able

to answer math problems. He would paw out the answers to questions on the wooden floor of his stall. The horse's trainer would always be present, but was closely scrutinized to make sure that he was not cueing the animal. People were amazed. One day the owner was put behind a screen during a question, and the horse could not answer correctly. The horse had learned to pick up on a subtle thumb movement by his owner. John Forbes told me that story. He also told me I was different from that owner, in that I could communicate with a horse on a much deeper level than simple visual cues. John believed I was the real thing, and that made me believe.

"Your relationship with Steve isn't good business," John told me. "It's not fair to our clients. Not only do they have to assess your riding abilities, but they also have to judge whether their trainer is unbiased. Julie, if you start losing, you'll be the scapegoat, not the horse, and we're going to be hard pressed to defend our position as good trainers, because the owner will have license to say that we are not paying attention strictly to your riding abilities." I told John that I didn't care. "Do you love him?" John asked. I answered yes. "Enough not to ride any horses in this outfit that he trains?" "I don't love him that much," I answered.

Several of John's owners threated to pull their horses from his barn. They didn't like girls, specifically Julie Krone, and said it was either me or them. It was a difficult decision for John, and he had to weigh the factors. Was I really good enough for him to risk the loss of additional clients? Would the clients who left him begin a trend, until he had lost his best horses? Was I loyal and dedicated to his barn? John also was receiving fan letters from people who wrote things like "It

A mother's love. Julie
takes a nap in the arms
of her mother, Judi.
(Don Krone)

Her first ride — Julie
aboard the family dog,
Twiggy. *(Don Krone)*

Above, left: Julie at age four with her pony, Dixie. *(Don Krone)*

Above: A five-year-old Julie with her first riding trophy and Dixie. *(Don Krone)*

Left: Filly, the diabolical pony, and a determined Julie. *(Don Krone)*

Training her first ponies — Julie with
Filly and Ibn. *(Don Krone)*

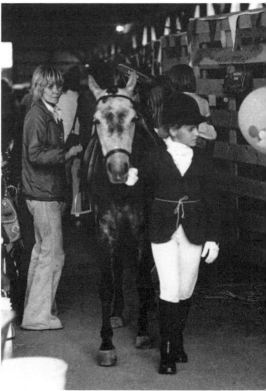

Winter in Eau Claire, Michigan. Julie
mushing her Great Dane. *(Don Krone)*

Right: The Berrien County Youth Fair.
Julie before her first dressage class — she
won. *(Don Krone)*

Julie and Arabian, Ralphy, practicing their tricks. *(Don Krone)*

Julie, age ten, and Filly. *(Don Krone)*

Judi with her Great
Danes. *(Don Krone)*

Clowning around —
Julie with childhood
friend Tracey Hanner.
(Don Krone)

Julie and brother Don-
nie playing cowboys and
Indians. *(Don Krone)*

Julie, age twenty-five, with Dixie. *(Don Krone)*

The early days — Julie racing at the Michigan fair tracks. *(Don Krone)*

Left: Best friend Lori Probst Skinner and Julie at the first race Lori attended. Julie won on Gaily Gaily. *(Don Krone)*

Julie and her father, Don Krone. *(Don Krone)*

Julie returns! July 25, 1990: Julie Krone returns to Monmouth Park Racetrack after an eight-month layoff. *(Equi-Photo/ Bill Denver)*

Julie meets one of her heroes, Bill "the Shoe" Shoemaker. *(Julie Krone Archive)*

Julie and David Letterman chat on his television show in 1989. *(Courtesy National Broadcasting Company)*

(*From left*) Trainer John Forbes, Julie, and agent Larry "Snake" Cooper discussing Julie's decision to become a New York rider. (*Julie Krone Archive*)

(*From left*) Trainer Bill Mott and owners Bert and Diana Firestone talk to Julie at Saratoga. (*Julie Krone Archive*)

Julie in a 1992 race aboard #10 at Saratoga. *(Barbara D. Livingston)*

A victorious leap off Rubiano after a 1992 race at Saratoga. *(Barbara D. Livingston)*

The Belmont — Julie
races to success aboard
Colonial Affair.
(Barbara D. Livingston)

1993: Julie wins five in
one day at Saratoga.
(Barbara D. Livingston)

Peter Rabbit and Julie win the 1994 USET Challenge of Champions.
(Barbara D. Livingston)

Julie and Colonial Affair in the winner's circle after the Belmont Stakes.
(Barbara D. Livingston)

Christopher Reeve and Julie smile for photographers after the USET Challenge of Champions. *(Barbara D. Livingston)*

Julie with jockey Angel Cordero. *(Barbara D. Livingston)*

The Female Sport Athlete of the Year — Julie Krone at the ESPY awards. *(Anita and Steve Shevett)*

Julie poses with hockey star Wayne Gretzky in 1991. *(Julie Krone Archive)*

Julie recuperating after a near-tragic 1993 Saratoga spill. *(Barbara D. Livingston)*

Julie back in the seat again, April 21, 1994. *(Barbara D. Livingston)*

hurts so bad to see you losing when you could be winning if you dropped Julie Krone."

There's a saying at the racetrack, "No jockey is worth an owner." A lot of trainers believe that they can always go to the jocks' room and get another jockey, but finding another owner is more difficult. John ignored what everyone considered common sense when he decided to keep me on. He risked his reputation when he made that decision. But in the end, we made the owners that pulled their horses regret their decision.

John didn't just care about the races I rode for him. He cared about my career as a jockey. John knew that my career couldn't evolve if I rode only his horses. He worked to get other trainers and their owners to ride me. After a race at Meadowlands, John approached me in the paddock with a trainer who had a half-dozen horses. John saw an opportunity to introduce me and to get me another barn to ride for. "So, Julie," John said seriously as I peeled my goggles back and wiped the dirt from my mouth, "how was the track?" The idea was that I'd say something really intelligent and impressive about the conditions that day. I had no idea who the guy with John was, and replied with a sideways grin, "I dunno." The trainer walked away in disgust.

I wish I had recognized how much John tried to do for me. I was twenty years old and still hadn't developed the ability to identify or acknowledge the gifts I was given. John Forbes taught me about sacrifice, loyalty, and empathy, and he and his wife, Vicki, welcomed me into their lives, home, and family. And when I had my first broken heart they stood right in my corner, ready to catch me when I fell.

– 10 –

LOVE LOSS

ONE MORNING STEVE Brown no longer loved me. It came out of the blue, and I was devastated. "I'm going to wrap my car around a telephone pole and put myself out of this misery," I told Vicki Forbes. "I just want to die," I cried to John. Both listened, sometimes in the darkness of night, sometimes in the weak light of dawn. Either one could have said, "Julie, I'm tired, I'll see you in the morning," but they didn't. When I'd call at two a.m., Vicki would talk to me about the weather, her daughter, Annie, or a race. She was very patient, kind, and sweet. John, too, spent long hours trying to help me. To this day I credit John, Vicki, and my new agent, Larry Cooper, for dragging me out of the deepest depression of my life.

Steve Brown was my first true love — and my first experience with romantic rejection. When he broke up with me, my reaction, given that I truly believed I would have chosen riding his horses over our relationship (if John Forbes had forced me to) surprised even me. I did everything I could to improve myself, to somehow become a different person so Steve would love me again. It didn't work. One day I found myself crumpled on the kitchen floor, crying about Steve and wishing I were dead. "I'm going to kill myself," I sobbed to no one in particular. But someone inside me answered, "That's a really stupid idea."

I picked myself off the floor about the same time that Steve got a new girlfriend. She didn't feel comfortable with me riding any of the horses he trained, and Steve and I no longer felt comfortable working together. So for the year of 1984–85, I rode only a few horses in New Jersey for John Forbes's stable. Although John tried to get me on some of his horses, the ones Steve didn't train, there wasn't much he could do for me. I had begun a losing streak, 0 for 80, and John's owners didn't want to ride me anymore. I couldn't blame them.

I was pathetic. I'd sit in the jocks' room at Keystone and watch the horses I had ridden just months before win race after race. My boyfriend had broken up with me, my cat had disappeared, and all the horses I used to ride were winning while I was bogged down in a disastrous losing streak. Depression is a mild word for what I felt. For six months I was unable to do anything more than go through the motions. I didn't even have enough energy to shower or eat regularly. Then Mary Ann Alligood, a fellow jockey, forced me to take a look at myself.

Mary Ann Alligood is a great rider, self-raised, self-trained, strong, and very intense. Though we had not yet become good friends, Mary Ann and I had ridden together in New Jersey before Steve and I broke up. "God, Julie," she said to me one afternoon, "you're so pitiful, even I feel sorry for you." She gave me a hug, which was rather out of character for her, and the gesture touched me. Boy, I must be in pretty bad shape for Mary Ann to feel so sorry for me, I thought. That was the day I began to come alive again.

Snake — Larry Cooper — helped me, too. He became my agent in 1983, after I had been the leading rider at Atlantic City for two consecutive meets. I'd been waiting for Chick to come to New Jersey to represent me, but he was unable to leave Maryland, so he suggested that I hire Snake. Unfortunately, that was around the time Steve and I broke up and I began my losing streak.

After my conversation with Mary Ann, Snake and I left Keystone and went to the track at Garden State Park. We spent hours every day trying to figure out why I was still losing. "Maybe I should shorten my stirrups, eat different food, go to Kentucky or some state where no one knows me." "Maybe we should get up earlier to talk to trainers," Snake suggested. We did, but only succeeded in ending the torture of rejection earlier each morning. They still didn't want to ride me. I was untouchable.

- 11 -

SNAKE, STREAKS, AND SUCCESS

"You can't be lucky that long, and you can't be that stupid," John Forbes said of Larry Cooper. A good jockey's agent has to appear uncalculating while somewhere, in the back of his mind, he's thinking. An agent has to be believable, even when he's lying. And sometimes he has to lie in order to get his jockey on the best horses. Most important, a good agent has to have the ability to make a furious trainer ride his jockey again. Snake Cooper is a natural. He's great with people, and no one can stay mad at him for long, even me.

Together, Snake (the nickname was given to him as a child, and its origin is cloudy) and I make a great team. It's his job to get me on the best horses, and at times to spin (drop) a trainer whose horse he's promised to ride, in order to get me on a better horse. I'm not a part of that side of riding. Snake and I have two separate roles that work extremely well together. If he spins someone, I don't know about it. And, when I find out, I can react in a genuine manner, especially if I feel Snake was wrong. I can't count the number of trainers who have threatened never to ride me again after Snake has spun them on the day of a race. And it's impossible to remember how many times I've dressed Snake up one side and down the other for spinning trainers. But in the end, it's business. Snake takes care of his, and once I'm on a horse, I do the rest.

Throughout my losing streak Snake stuck with me. We never blamed each other; we just kept trying to improve. After we moved from Keystone to Garden State Park in Cherry Hill, New Jersey, I began to win a few races. Finally, Glenn Lane and Dennis Herd approached me in what became the turning point of my career. Glenn Lane is an owner, and his partner, Dennis Herd, is a trainer. Together they have a unique racing stable. Unique because it has a set philosophy for their horses — ride them on the rail so they travel the shortest possible route around the track. Jockeys tend to ride naturally, getting out free from the pack when they can and doing what the horse wants. But not the jockeys that rode for Glenn and Dennis. And if a jockey heeded their advice, regardless of whether or not the horse won, Glenn and Dennis were happy with his trip.

In the winter of 1986 Glenn offered me a one-shot deal to ride one of his horses in one race, because his regular jockey, Chris Antley, had chosen a different horse for that race. A racing stable guarantees that a great jockey is continuously available to ride by offering him a choice of the stable's horses. That ensures the jockey that he will get to ride live (successful) horses and gives him incentive to adapt to a stable's racing style. It was strange to have Chris Antley, who had looked up to me, now surpassing me as Glenn and Dennis's main rider.

I was happy for Chris. He is a phenomenal athlete and a wonderful jockey to watch because of his natural ability. Throughout my whole life I know that I will come across athletes who are greater or lesser than I am. If they are lesser, I will be kind and empathetic, and if they are greater, I'm determined to learn from their successes. But it would be dishonest to say that Chris's success didn't eat at me a little. In my heart I was proud of him, and at the same time I was professionally jealous.

Glenn and Dennis's offer to let me ride for them in one race was atypical. When a main rider isn't available for a race, the stable will usually put a bug rider on the horse. Bug riders do what they're told, which for Glenn and Dennis meant staying on the rail, and are eager to learn from the experience. It's very rewarding for an apprentice rider to learn how to save ground by staying on the rail, and to place themselves in a pocket and then make their horse charge at the end of the race. It also makes that rider look really smart. For a month, Snake and I had spoken with Glenn and Dennis, trying to get on their horses. Even though it was a one-shot deal we accepted their offer.

I won the race, beating Chris Antley by a nose. When the meet at Garden State Park ended, Dennis and Glenn asked me if I wanted to ride all the horses in their barn. Just like that, my slump was over and I began slowly to rebuild my career. The entire situation taught me two valuable lessons: First, to never give up, not even when I was 0 for 80, because there was no way to know when a Glenn Lane, Dennis Herd, or Bud Delp was watching. Second, that clinging to past loves, dreams, and successes stymies any movement toward the future. Only by letting go could I continue to develop both as a person and as a jockey.

During my slump, John Forbes had given me many books and self-help tapes. One particular passage in *Illusions*, by Richard Bach, reflected my own difficulties and helped me to let go.

> *"Once there lived a village of creatures along the bottom of a great crystal river. . . .*
>
> *The current of the river swept silently over them all — young and old, rich and poor, good and evil, the current going its own way, knowing only its own crystal self. . . .*
>
> *Each creature in its own manner clung tightly to the twigs and rocks of the river bottom, for clinging was their way of life, and resisting the current was what each had learned from birth. . . .*
>
> *But one creature said at last, "I am tired of clinging. Though I cannot see it with my eyes, I trust that the current knows where it is going. I shall let go, and let it take me where it will. Clinging, I shall die of boredom. . . ."*
>
> *The other creatures laughed and said, "Fool! Let go, and that current you worship will throw you tumbled and smashed across the rocks, and you will die quicker than of boredom! . . ."*

But the one heeded them not, and taking a breath did
let go, and at once was tumbled and smashed by the
current across the rocks. . . .

Yet in time, as the creature refused to cling again, the
current lifted him free from the bottom, and he was
bruised no more. . . .

And the creatures downstream, to whom he was a
stranger, cried, "See, a miracle! A creature like
ourselves, yet he flies! . . ."

And the one carried in the current said . . . , "The
river delights to lift us free, if only we dare let go. Our
true work is this voyage, this adventure."

The summer of 1986, Glenn and Dennis asked me to come to
Monmouth Park and ride all the horses in their barn. From
that moment on, every meet I rode I was one of the top two
riders. Their horses had quality, and were so competitive that
it was a real treat to ride them. And I learned a lot from Glenn
and Dennis, who had a very aggressive training style. I'd say,
"Glenn, this horse is really pulling on the left rein," and instead of trying to figure out exactly why the horse was pulling
left, Glenn would say, "So pull back on the right rein." At first
I'd look at him like he was crazy — you don't do that with
horses — but after a while I began to listen, and found his
advice sound. Glenn taught me not to be a victim. I took his
advice and applied it to every aspect of my life. But there are
times when being a victim is not a choice.

*   *   *

In 1986 my mother called the track and told me that she had
ovarian cancer. "Well, how are they going to fix it?" I immediately wanted to know. "It's pretty hard to fix," my mom
replied. She didn't tell me that the doctor she had seen had
closed her abdomen after his exploratory surgery and told her
that he couldn't do anything for her. The cancer was too advanced, he'd said. There wasn't a single organ in her abdominal
cavity that wasn't covered with stage IV cancer — the most
advanced form of the disease. The doctor instructed my mom
to get her affairs in order.

I asked for the name of Mom's doctor, and after we hung
up I called him. He explained that the survival rate for ovarian
cancer was poor, around two percent, and made her prognosis
sound pretty grim. Then the doctor told me she had less
than two years to live. Terrible thoughts raced through my
head — my mother would never see me get married, never play
with her grandchildren. . . .

She found a new oncologist, Dr. Linda Morgan, who at the
time worked at the University at Florida, Gainesville, hospital.
Initially, Mom was supposed to see the head of the women's
tumor department in Gainesville, but at the last minute, she
was switched to the second in command, Dr. Morgan. I truly
believe that switch saved her life.

Linda Morgan is a highly talented physician, who has not
only increased the survival rate of women with ovarian cancer,
but has also elevated its treatment to an art form. Dr. Morgan
immediately reduced the level of my mother's cancer to stage
III. She discovered that although all of Mom's abdominal organs were diseased, the cancer covered only the top of the

organs and hadn't penetrated them. Unlike the other doctors, Linda Morgan was optimistic. She immediately introduced Mom to a woman who had been diagnosed with ovarian cancer the year before Mom's diagnosis. That woman became an inspiration for my mother and at the same time let her know that in the next few years she would go through hell but that there was a light at the end of the tunnel.

And she did go through hell. Mom began with two months of chemotherapy. The chemotherapy made her quite sick, but it was the two ensuing surgeries that really threw her for a loop. They were the most horrible surgeries anyone could ever imagine. After two months of chemotherapy Mom's cancer cells had become soft, grape-sized masses. This new consistency made it easier for Dr. Morgan to remove them from Mom's intestines and organs. After an initial surgery Mom was given more cancer-killing drugs, and two months later had her second surgery to remove all the remaining cells. Basically, as she lay on the operating table, all her organs were removed, scraped clean, and placed back in her abdominal cavity. The ones that had become too diseased and damaged were removed. She was very sick after that surgery, and ten days later she became sicker when she began to take the "rad drugs," which are cancer-attacking drugs called "radical" because they are so strong.

I felt helpless. I would call my Mom and ask if there was anything I could do. She'd always say, "Yes, win races for me," in a voice thick with drugs and pain. So I did. Every day that I won, for almost a year, I'd call her and tell her about the race, blow by blow. At the end of each week, I'd Federal Express videotapes of my best races to her. Later I learned that Mom had shared those tapes with fellow patients, who gathered in the patients' lobby to watch Judi Krone's daughter. When a patient has chemotherapy and radiation they usually don't want to be around other people; they would just as soon stay in their room and try to sleep. Usually they feel sick most of the time, but it's still better for them if they can get out of their room. Those race tapes gave my mother a reason to get out of bed, and ended up creating a network of friends and supporters.

I was winning more and more, but I still felt powerless to help my mother. Dr. Morgan was continuing to battle the cancer with no holds barred. Mom spent ten months receiving massive doses of chemotherapy. During that time, the woman who had been her initial inspiration died from her cancer.

On August 19, 1987, I had a record day at Monmouth Park. Following each race, I ran past the first-aid room and yelled in to the doctor, my friend Angelo, to call my mom and tell her I won one. After my fourth win, Angelo began joking with my mom — "She's not done yet, Judi," he said. He was right. Angelo spoke with my mom six times that day — and by the time the races were over, I had equaled the track's single-day win record.

I can't emphasize enough how wonderful it is to have multiple-win days. I'll be the first to say that those days are a combination of a powerful stable, fantastic trainers, and the opportunities a winning jockey receives. The jockey has to work her butt off to put herself in a winning situation, but when she rides horses that have a high probability of winning and low odds, she is going to win more races. The secret of multiple-win days is to put all those factors together in one day. And when it happens, there is an unbelievable rush and a real sense of power.

By the end of August, 1987, I had become the second female rider to pass the 1,200 mark for career wins, joining P. J. Cooksey, and that year I became the first woman to win riding titles at major racetracks, with victories at Monmouth Park (130 wins) and Meadowlands (124 wins). I also set the Meadowlands record of six wins in a single night and then repeated that record on another night.

My mother left the hospital that winter and returned to her farm in Florida. Sometimes I wondered how she could sleep, knowing that the cancer could still come back, could still kill her. It's hard enough to sleep when everyday problems plague your mind, let alone when you have to wonder how many weeks you have left to live. Today there are only two people from mom's initial hospitalization who are still surviving ovarian cancer, and she is one of them.

One year before my mother's diagnosis of cancer, I had bought her a gray thoroughbred stallion for Valentine's Day, named It'saGrayIssue, and had him trucked to her farm. She still remembers watching the big gray with black mane and tail come down her driveway, his forelock stirring in the breeze. A year later, his first foal, Petey, was born on Easter Sunday. Mom watched the birth on a cool Florida morning. The mare and GrayIssue stood beneath an enormous tree whose boughs were draped with deep green moss. Together they cleaned off the foal. He was a perfect little chestnut boy with four white socks and a big white blaze. The sun rose behind the three horses, creating a dazzling silhouette and reminding my mother of the glory of life. A month after that, Mom had found out she had cancer.

"Well, you can't die now, because you have to train that

foal to be a jumper for me," I told her several months after the foal, whom I named Peter Rabbit, was born. So my mother set out to train a horse for her daughter. And she continued that training for the two years she battled for her life, especially when she returned to her ranch after her hospitalization and ten months of chemotherapy. I believe that training kept her spirits from waning after the long battle and helped her regain her love of life, allowing her to once again work her special brand of magic with horses.

Petey was a very spunky colt, with a bit of a mean streak. There were days when my mother would fall down while lunging him, days where his spirit threatened to defeat her own. But that horse's strength just made my mother more resolved. Secretly I was glad Petey was difficult to train. That meant it would take my mother longer, and ultimately she'd have to live longer to get the job done. My mother always got the job done.

Today I joke that my mom's too stubborn and ornery to die of cancer. That cancer probably ran away from her. But for a few years I thought I might lose her. I believe that the horses and my success, as well as her own firm belief in God, helped her to fight, just as those elements helped me to struggle through my own fears about my mother's mortality.

"Everyone becomes religious in a foxhole," a friend of mine used to say. But I have always turned to God in both good and bad times. It is instinctive for me to thank God when things in my life go well, just as I turn to Him when things go wrong. My mother's cancer was no exception.

A lot of things have gone wrong in my life, and just as many have gone right. Throughout, I have never lost my faith. I'm very thankful that my mother's parents, Carl and Marguerite Weber, showed me at a young age how to love Jesus and put my faith in Him. Although I always went to Bible summer school as a child, and enjoyed coloring pictures of Jesus and learning that God was good and helped it rain, it was my grandparents who opened the door of my heart to the joy of faith.

I spent several weeks in March, 1974, visiting my grandparents in Tampa. It was a novel experience. Not just because I traveled to Florida by myself or because I was surrounded by older people instead of my usual young playmates and assortment of animals, but because religion played an integral role in my grandparents' lives.

During the week, I attended the Baptist church with my grandparents and spent evenings listening to them discuss their love and faith with their friends. My grandmother and I attended Bible study, and I once said a prayer in front of her study group. The words flowed out of my mouth easily because I felt strength in my belief and my love, a strength that I drew upon naturally and have continued to draw upon.

I don't know if I could have survived my drug addiction, heartbreak, the trials and tribulations of becoming a jockey, and the subsequent accidents that left me battered and broken, without God's help. Just as I don't know if my mother would be alive today without His intervention.

There is a peace that pure faith gives that has allowed me and many of the ones I love to triumph against the odds, to look the Devil in the eye until he backs off and fades away.

- 12 -

PERSONAL GROWTH

I NEVER JUST sat back and enjoyed the winning. Racing isn't a sport where a rider can rest on her laurels. Winning three or even six races in one day only means something for the moment. After crossing the wire and spending a few minutes in the winner's circle, a rider has to change her silks for the next race, and then the next. The struggle to ride "live" horses never ends. The goal is to have a live one in every race, and that depends upon the relationships a jockey builds with owners and trainers.

There are always people who refuse to ride certain jockeys, who don't believe in that rider's skills or abilities. So every day after races, whether it was a good or a bad day, I try to track those people down, to try even harder to crack them. I tell them, "Look what I accomplished today. You should probably ride me." Even if they don't, I have a nice conversation with them and try to alter their perception of me. That's not so easy.

It was hard in the early days. Regardless of my successes in 1986 and 1987, I had a lot to learn.

"Don't you guys know anything? Maybe you should go to grooming school before you come to work for a trainer," I snapped at a groom who had not adjusted my saddle properly. It is a groom's responsibility to have a particular horse ready for a rider when she enters the barn. When I arrive at a barn to ride a horse in morning workouts, the groom should already have walked the horse out of the stall and down the shed row to loosen his muscles, put the saddle on, and adjusted the girth appropriately.

On that particular morning, I mounted my horse and discovered that the last horse that had worn the saddle was much larger than mine. So instead of riding down the shed row, adjusting my stirrups, wrapping my knot (fixing the reins with a knot at the appropriate length), and moving out to the track, I had to get off the horse, drop the girth on its elastic side, fix the yoke, pull the girth up, and then remount the horse. When a jockey is on a tight time schedule, those wasted minutes seem like hours.

I thought, Jeez, this groom has been with the horse for twenty-five minutes and he can't even adjust the girth correctly. That particular morning, the same problems had occurred with several of my horses. I was at the end of my rope, and took my anger out on that groom. After I breezed his horse, Pat McBurney, an assistant trainer for John Forbes, pulled me aside and said, "I really would feel more comfortable if you wouldn't talk to my help like that. That groom has only been on the job for a little while, and he's doing his very best. There's a lot to remember. He's trying, and he really likes horses. If he quits tomorrow because you yelled at him and made him feel stupid, who's going to take care of his four horses?"

I'd never looked at it that way. I just wanted everyone to do everything perfectly all the time. After talking with Pat, I apologized to his groom. "I'm really sorry," I said. "I was just so hyped up about riding horses that I never put myself in your shoes." Everyone has a lesser or greater job, but above everything is the responsibility to get along with people. That day I learned that not only did I have to communicate well with owners and trainers, as John Forbes had taught me, but that everyone in the barn was part of a team — trainers, owners, grooms, hot-walkers, . . . even me.

For the rest of the day I kept thinking, Gosh, it's terrible to treat someone like I had. I have continued to learn about being aware of others. The people at the racetrack are the ones responsible for educating me. John Forbes taught me about friendship, and Pat McBurney showed me how to be empathetic. In the end, it has nothing to do with racehorses or racing. It's all about friendship and working happily with other people. Riding for me is not so much a business as it is a way of life.

Every new lifestyle has to be learned. The lifestyle of the racetrack was no different. In the mid-eighties I was becoming a success, and at times the attention overwhelmed me. I was a little girl from Eau Claire, Michigan, riding racehorses worth $250,000, meeting and mingling with wealthy owners, and beginning to feel my oats. Just as I had to learn how to treat the grooms in the barn, I had to learn how to work with my fellow jockeys.

"Did you see my race? It was incredible — beat him by a nose! That was my fourth winner today. . . . Did you see it, did ya?" The words would bubble out of my mouth as I entered the female jockeys' room. "Hey," I'd say to another jockey who had been in the race, "your riding position was too high; you need to lower your butt." It took a few years for me to develop an understanding of how those women who were less successful felt. I eventually became a sympathetic and empathetic person, and while it sounds strange that those traits had to be learned, in my case they did. I was brought up wild. My only concerns were the animals, the dogs, cats, and horses. My education at home revolved solely around their welfare. All the rest, the people skills, were summed up in the realistic words of my mother — "Life is tough. Deal with it."

In January, 1994, I visited friends in the jocks' room at Gulfstream Park in Florida. As I sat talking with Donna Barton, an apprentice jockey burst into the room. Something had gone wrong during her race, and she was recounting the action in a high-pitched whine. I stopped her and said, "What I'm about to tell you could be completely wrong for you, but I'm just giving you my opinion based on my experience. First, lower your voice. Whatever happened out there, you're going to have to explain it to your trainer. If you're hysterical, he's not going to understand you or believe a word you say. . . ." After I left the room I felt that old pang of worry. Had I again overstepped my bounds and put in my two cents where it wasn't wanted?

"Julie, I have something to tell you," Donna Barton said at dinner the following evening. "Remember what you told that apprentice jockey yesterday?" she began. Oh, no, I thought, she's going to tell me to keep my mouth shut. "Well, two races later another jockey came into the room with a similar problem. I said, 'I'm going to give you a piece of advice that Julie Krone gave to an apprentice jockey. First, lower your voice. . . .' " Man, that made me feel good.

– 13 –

DIABOLICAL DIVA

A DIABOLICAL RIDER. That's what they began to call me in the late 1980s as my success escalated. I was uncomfortable defining my riding style then, and still am today. A jockey is nothing in racing until all the facts and figures are in and her career is finished. Until that moment, she just has to keep riding her best. Diabolical rider? I don't know, that seems to connote being conniving in a negative sense, but smart rider, that label feels more comfortable.

What appears diabolical in a race can be translated into savvy, the ability to communicate with a horse. The first thing I do when I ride a racehorse is ask the trainer what he expects. For example, suppose a trainer tells me his horse is definitely a live horse but tends to bear on one rein to avoid other riders. That means the horse doesn't make the turn properly and could end up going very wide. Now I know where to be careful during the race. Or the trainer might say that the horse breaks early and is too aggressive, and he wants to teach him how to pace himself. He would ask that at the start of the race I put my horse behind some others to relax him and conserve energy, and that I make my break at the three-eighths pole (three eighths of a mile left in the race).

A few days before a race, I breeze the horse, get to know him. I place my hands and distribute my weight in ways that make him run better. If he's a nervous horse, I put my hands back by his withers, only pull a tiny bit when he pulls, give and relax when he gives and relaxes, and make sure I don't squeeze him with my legs or move my arms too much. There are twenty different movements I'll try in my first thirty seconds on that horse. When I find something that works, that brings him back between my hands and legs, I remember to use that movement during the race and hope that the horse can remember it too.

Before I race that particular horse, I spend time in the jockeys' room handicapping (rating the quality of horses in the race based on their past performances). Every horse has a different running style, and it's important to understand each horse in order to know the best spot to place my mount. If the trainer told me that his horse needs to relax at the start of the race, I try to find out which horses are quick early and like to race close to the lead, and then I plan to place my horse behind them. The last question I ask myself is What do I want to accomplish in this race for myself and my horse? I take that answer and mix it with what the trainer wants to accomplish, so that everyone will be happy.

When the gate clangs open and my horse begins to grab the

turf in an effort to get out in front, I put my hands on his neck and he comes back to me, relaxing instead of going off on his own. He remembered. We move behind the two quick horses, biding our time in a covered position. A horse at the start of a race is like a full balloon. With each stride, he loses air. The least amount of energy he has to use in the start will help him later. I always try to make sure my horse has enough energy to finish, enough air left to cross the wire. And if I don't need to use the whip, I don't. A horse's trip is more enjoyable if I can coax him forward by pushing gently with my hands.

At the three-eighths pole I ease my horse out a little bit, let him see daylight. When a horse sees daylight, it's almost like a new race for him; he wants to go. Since I've kept him calm most of the way, he has a lot of energy left. He passes those two quick horses, who are starting to tire, moves to the lead, and crosses the wire first. As I slow him, I begin to pat his neck and tell him what a good boy he has been. Even if we hadn't won, I would have stroked my horse and spoken softly, kindly into his ears. If a horse enjoys his race, he's going to try even harder the next time.

Of course, jockeys don't always win. And while that is the main goal, when I don't win a race I try to look at all the good things that happened throughout the effort. If my horse bided his time, conserved energy, ran well down the stretch, had a clean race, or was good in the starting gate, I know I can build on those positive elements. Each horse I ride is an investment — the investment of the owner, trainer, and grooms, as well as an investment in my own success. Even if my horse doesn't win, I know that I'll ride him again (there are some horses that have been ridden in their entire career only by me) and when he does win, I'll make sure that it is the right kind of win, one where he learns and has an enjoyable time.

That's it. That's my whole strategy: to be smart and educated about options during a race, to treat my horse like a valuable commodity, to listen to the trainer, and to trust in my own ability to communicate with my horse. To be a "diabolical rider," and to be successful in that effort, would require a type of consistency in riding that just isn't there. There are some riders who have particular habits or styles and some who are totally inconsistent in their form. Add those riders to ten horses who may or may not react to their efforts, and it is impossible to have a strategy that is even close to "diabolical." Mostly I just worry about keeping myself and my horse safe, not who I'm going to try to push to the rail or box in (trap behind my horse). Those things just happen. And when I do find that I've boxed someone in, I may use that to my advantage only to end up boxed behind another horse I thought was going to run faster.

There are no guarantees in racing, except that every jockey's life rests in the leather reins of her fellow jockeys' callused hands. It is not smart to be a diabolical rider in the negative sense of the word. To keep some sort of peace with all the jockeys is to protect yourself and your horse. Granted, there are situations that become personal. Situations where a few jockeys will jeopardize the rest because of a grudge against one rider.

My early career was marred by several of those incidents, which I am not proud of or able to excuse. The only thing I can say in my own defense is that I was the first female jockey to really threaten the positions of male jockeys, and some of those men just didn't want to be beaten by a little girl. I was also struggling to find a place in a sport that had few openings for women.

When grudges occur and a jockey begins to fight another rider on the turf, a few jockeys will approach the offending jockey after a race and say, "Play your games somewhere else, not out on the track when we're behind you and could be killed." Trainers will also speak with the jockey and threaten not to ride him if his actions jeopardize the soundness of their horse and the lives of other riders. More often than not the offender straightens out his act. Usually it's a young rider who hasn't learned that jockeys might ride for different trainers but are ultimately in the game together.

Once I realized that I was in the same situation as the next guy, riding became easier. It's humiliating to get boxed in by other riders. It makes the jockey look stupid, angers the trainer and owner, and doesn't allow a horse to run at its full potential. Personally, it hurts my feelings to be boxed in or outridden, but it happens to me, and I often do it to other riders. I make sure, though, that when I out-ride another athlete I do it with respect and never rub his face in the loss. Still, there's no guarantee how another jockey will accept defeat.

– 14 –

FIGHTS, FIGHTS, FIGHTS

In 1986, AFTER a race at Monmouth Park, I had one of my most infamous altercations, with a jockey named Miguel Rujano. I was leading rider in Monmouth, and Rujano was a jockey who didn't ride much. He was too heavy, and had to spend a lot of time reducing his weight with Lasix, using the sweat box, and starving himself. The week before our fight, Rujano had lost a race to Joe Rocco, a cool little jockey from Brooklyn. As the two pulled up their horses, Rujano made a crack about Joe's pregnant wife and suggested that maybe he (Rujano) had fathered the child. Joe leapt off his horse and the two men fought.

The following week at the races, I pulled out of the gate and my horse drifted in one step toward Rujano's mount. I immediately straightened out my horse and went forward. I won the race by a large distance and Rujano finished quite a way back. As I pulled my horse up, Rujano trotted up next to me and hit me right in the face with his whip. I had my goggles down, so the whip wrapped around the front of my face and caught the lobe of my ear. I remember thinking, Wow, that guy just hit me with a whip! I was flabbergasted, and just turned my horse around and rode back to the scales. As I was riding, I felt something sticky on my neck. I reached up and my hand filled with blood. The whip had split my ear open.

I'm going to kill him! was my first thought as I jumped off my horse and walked with my saddle to the scales to weigh in. I threw my saddle down and ran over to Rujano, who was talking on the telephone to the stewards to claim a foul against me. I took a punch at him. My fist glanced off the side of his face, and he fell into a cooler, dumping water everywhere. The clerk at the scales held me and ordered Rujano to return to the jocks' room. The officials reviewed the tape and a few minutes later ruled that there was no foul. I went to the winner's circle to have my picture taken, and then walked back to the jockeys' room. Rujano was waiting for me by the swimming pool. He grabbed me and threw me into the pool. Then he jumped in after me and tried to hold me under the water. He tried to drown me, although later he told the stewards that he just wanted to make me swallow a little water. I got away and swam to the side of the pool. Once out, I grabbed a pool chair and threw it at Rujano. I was hysterical — scared, angry, feeling crazy.

The next day the senior steward, Sam Boulmetis Jr., called me into his office. He had already suspended Rujano, who had failed a drug test. I expected Sam to comfort me and say that the incident was all Rujano's fault. But Sam didn't care about Rujano. "Sit down, Julie," he ordered in a serious tone. I sat. Sam commenced to tell me that I was becoming a leading rider,

116 * JULIE KRONE

and that he would not accept a little girl fighting at his race-track. I was speechless. How could he yell at me, when Rujano was the one who had attacked me, had started everything. Sam said he wanted to see me move to the next level. He wanted me to become a professional. He said that if I was ever caught fighting again at any racetrack with anybody for any reason he would suspend me. I was furious with him. "Julie," he said as I left, "you can ride out there on the racetrack like a man, you're tougher than any rider I've ever seen, but you cannot act like a man when you get off the horses. You have to act like a lady."

He was right, but it took me a while to learn that lesson.

The fight with Yves Turcotte started when I came up next to him halfway through a race and he was so angered by my move that he took his whip out and hit my horse across the face with it. It made me crazy that someone would hit a horse on purpose like that. When we got back to the scales I threw my saddle down and pushed him, yelling at the same time that he had hit my horse. Yves didn't fight back, but we both got into trouble — Yves for hitting a horse, me for hitting a jockey.

Jake Nied was not a well known or competitively successful jockey. After a race where he felt my horse had impeded him, Nied grabbed me by the shirt and broke the necklace I was wearing. My horse was wearing a burr (a brush cut into a circle) on the left side of his head to keep him from lugging or pulling in. (A burr isn't painful; it feels like a hairbrush and just reminds the horse not to pull.) As I rode past Jake Nied, the burr slipped off my horse's head and he began to drift in on Nied. I pulled my horse over, but there was no way to keep him from drifting. A moment later we were past Nied with no harm done. After the race Nied approached me and yelled, "Don't you ever do that again!" I tried to explain to him that the horse would have drifted in on any rider at that moment, and that I hadn't tried to impede him. Nied attacked me anyway. That's when my instincts as a little sister kicked in, and I broke away. I was pretty upset. It's frightening to have a guy screaming and grabbing you, but I didn't fight back. I heard Sam's words in my head, and I just walked away.

Sometimes I didn't just walk away, I ran. In a race at Keystone I couldn't guide my horse properly, and we impeded Mary Ann Alligood. "I'm going to get you," she shouted as we slowed our horses after the wire. She was really mad, and I was afraid of her. I rode quickly to the scales, pulled my saddle off, weighed in, and then raced to the first-aid room to hide. When Mary Ann came back to the jockeys' room she couldn't find me. Eventually she asked the clerk of scales where I was, and he told her I was hiding in the first-aid room. "That's good," she told the clerk, "because that's where I was going to send her anyway." By then Mary Ann had cooled off a bit.

I snuck back to the jocks' room and peeked around the corner of the doorway. Mary Ann was grinning. "You're lucky," she said with a wag of her finger, "that you stayed out of my way for a while." She didn't have to tell me that. I was more afraid of her than of any male jockey. Mary Ann was one tough woman — she'd been fighting to be a successful jockey years before I'd begun my own battle.

In 1988 at Garden State Park, jockey Armando Marquez reached over during a race and grabbed my reins, preventing my horse from winning. Marquez claimed that he had been throwing his crosses (spreading his hands apart so his reins would separate and then come together) to tell his horse to go forward. His hand, he said, had accidentally gotten caught in my reins. Although no one will ever know his intentions for certain, it's a bit hard to believe Marquez's story, especially since the replay showed that he had clearly grabbed my horse's rein. His actions could have seriously hurt me, my horse, or the other riders on the track. After the wire, I felt an instant red rage wash over my body. I tried to remember what Sam had said to me, that he wanted more out of me than other jockeys, and I knew that if I fought with Marquez I would seriously disappoint Sam. In the end I kept my composure. Marquez was disqualified and suspended, and I was proud of myself for avoiding a fight.

It was bad enough that I got into yet another fight with a jockey, but worse because it happened at Meadowlands. On Saturday, September 23, 1989, in the seventh race of the Meadowlands' Glassboro Handicap, Joey Bravo and I got into a prolonged scuffle. I was riding a horse named Mosquera, who was the favorite. Bravo was on Kute Kelly, a ten to one shot. In the middle of the race, Bravo began to ride me unnecessarily tight. I was in a dangerous position — my filly was too close to the fence — and I screamed, "No, Joe! Don't do it! No, no, no!" He pushed me in closer, and I reached over and hit him. He pulled his whip through to the left and hit my horse in the face, then moved in farther, making the situation tighter. "You jerk," I yelled. "Why are you doing this?"

When we crossed the wire, we were already pushing at each other. At the scales I pushed him, and he took a swing at me and connected. I fought back, and finally a trainer jumped in and threw Bravo to the ground. When he regained his feet, I ran over and pushed him into the metal railing. It's impossible to know who knocked his teeth out, the trainer or me.

The stewards, including Sam, fined us both and suspended me for fifteen days. I was upset, but knew that I needed the time off. I'd been riding fourteen horses a day for two months straight with only one day or night off a week. I was fried. Maybe if I hadn't been so tired, I wouldn't have reacted as violently to Bravo's dangerous riding. He was a young jockey, reckless and too aggressive, and hadn't learned not to put other jockeys in dangerous positions. I doubt if he would repeat his actions today, just as I wouldn't react in the same manner.

I've been a jockey for fourteen years. The fights I've had have certainly been well documented, but that documentation overshadows what happens between jockeys ninety-nine percent of the time. No one writes about the jockeys who teach each other how to switch their whips, or who comfort each other after a bad race and sincerely congratulate each other following a success. No one notices how many jockeys visit their friends in the hospital after bad spills, or the cards sent and letters written. But because I was something of an anomaly in the eighties, my escapades received undue attention, and unfortunately detracted from the sport.

In those early years, there were reporters who wrote that I got into fights with other jockeys because I was a girl and felt the need to be tough to prove myself. They wrote that the male jockeys had trouble accepting me, that they made things difficult for me. But I think the person who made things toughest on me was me. I was overflowing with drive and determination, and nothing was going to get in the way of my success.

When I became a successful jockey — more successful than any other woman who had previously been involved in the sport and more successful than most men — there were no female role models to show me how to act. In the beginning I had to be scrappy and aggressive to be taken seriously by trainers, owners, and other jockeys. I acted like a typical tough guy, not a girl. When success came, I had to learn that I was finally being afforded the luxury of being a woman. I'd proved myself, proved to the world that male or female, the only jockeys that counted were the ones who performed.

In the old days I would never have worn a skirt to the races. No makeup, no special hairstyle. Those things were viewed as unprofessional by other jockeys and the trainers and owners. Then I became a successful jockey, and all of a sudden people like Sam were telling me that *I* was a role model, that I had to act like a lady. Wait a minute, I thought, I had to be tough to get where I am; why are the rules changing?

I was also living like a transient, moving from state to state, racetrack to racetrack. I had no roots, no home. There were times when, overwhelmingly tired of the travel, I felt as if I had no ties, no responsibilities to anyone but myself, the horses, trainers, and owners. It would take a bit longer before I would settle down, buy the farm of my dreams, and call somewhere home. And when I did, a lot of my frustrations dissipated.

Most important, I learned that no one is ever on the right side in a fight.

– 15 –

THE SHOE

DON'T FOOL WITH ME was the name of the horse I rode in 1988 in a match race against Bill Shoemaker, the winningest jockey of all time. The Shoe isn't just the winningest jockey; he had been one of my heroes since the moment I decided to pursue a riding career. And now there I was at Canterbury Downs in Minnesota riding head to head with the Shoe before a crowd of 9,487 fans.

The match race was one mile on a turf course. The horses, Don't Fool With Me and Shoe's mount, Dakota Slew, were chosen by Canterbury Downs's director of racing, Tom Knust. He did a great job, because the horses had almost identical abilities, and the result was that the race couldn't have been closer. But I had two advantages over Shoe. First, I drew the post one position, which gave me the shortest trip around the course. Second, I knew that the first turn at Canterbury Downs would come up sharp, because I had ridden over the course the previous month in the Jockey Challenge race. Had the match race been a normal race with other jockeys, I probably would have told Shoe about the latter advantage.

When we broke from the gate we were head to head. I had a slight lead after entering the first turn. Dakota Slew didn't make the turn smoothly. On the backstretch I increased my lead by a length and a half. But in the stretch Shoe came back. We were riding tight together, and I lost the lead briefly at the one-eighth-mile pole. With a sixteenth left, I pushed on Don't Fool With Me's neck, asking for anything he had in reserve. He had just enough. We beat Shoe by a nose.

It was a strange feeling. Strange, but at the same time wonderful. Bill Shoemaker had meant so much to me throughout my early riding career. As I sat in the winner's circle, I remembered the hours I'd spent trying to emulate his style as I raced Ralphy down the dirt roads in Michigan. I remembered poring over his book with my mother in the dim light of our farmhouse, trying to figure out what made The Shoe so great. And although I beat him that day, he was a wonderful sportsman. In the end, the opportunity to be in a duel with him, to ride beside him down the stretch, was overwhelming. The fact that I won was just icing on the cake.

Sometimes there is no icing on the cake. Sometimes an opportunity is just that, an opportunity. And no matter how hard a jockey tries, there are times when she can't make it golden.

It wasn't that Laffit Pincay didn't want to ride Forty Niner. Any jockey in his right mind would have practically killed to ride such a great athlete. But Laffit Pincay chose to honor the

1988 strike by New York jockeys, who were trying to get a higher percentage of money for the horses in second and third place. He refused to come to New York to ride Forty Niner in the Metropolitan Mile, a huge stakes race. His decision was an honorable one.

Seth Hancock, the owner of Forty Niner and Claiborne Farm, and Forty Niner's trainer, Woody Stephens, decided that if Laffit Pincay wouldn't come to New York for the Met, they wouldn't allow him to ride their horse in the Breeders' Cup Classic at Churchill Downs. The Breeders' Cup is thoroughbred racing's year-end championship consisting of seven races held on one day at a different track each year. Purses and awards for the day total $10 million. Hancock and Stephens refused to ride Pincay, and that's where I came in. I'd ridden Forty Niner at Monmouth, so Woody Stephens called Snake and asked if I wanted to ride his horse in the Breeders' Cup. Did I!

For years I had been trying to ride as much as possible for Woody Stephens. He's an extraordinary trainer — if Woody told me I could ride the goat in his shed row, I'd say, "Okay, where is he?" Riding for Woody and Claiborne Farm was a big step in my career. Some jockeys wait their whole life for the opportunity to ride for such a powerful stable with such well-bred horses. I was getting a shot early in my career. Did I want to ride their horse? You bet.

The pressure was on. I was the first woman to ever ride in the Breeders' Cup. I was aboard a Triple Crown winner, surrounded by an enormous crowd and a large group of reporters who all wanted to know how I felt. I felt good. Nervous, but good.

Before the race, Forty Niner warmed up wonderfully. I had already placed second in a juvenile filly race that day, and I was feeling strong and confident. Forty Niner and I were in sync, and at six P.M., as dusk settled and the outdoor lights at the Downs track lit up, I rode Forty Niner onto the track. When the starting gates clanged open, we exploded. I moved to the inside, tracking Alysheba, winner of a 1988 Eclipse Award (thoroughbred racing's year-end awards honoring the top horses). The roar from the crowd was deafening. As we came up on the turn, there was a television camera beneath a light, and it cast a large shadow on the inside of the brightly lit track. Forty Niner saw the shadow and leapt into the air in an effort to clear whatever obstacle he thought was in front of him. Then he took a half step behind Alysheba and slapped the ground with his hooves three times. He began to slow, and did a strange hop. I thought Forty Niner had hurt himself, and for a moment I sat still on his back. I didn't pull him up drastically, I just wanted to be certain that he wasn't hurt. Three more strides and Forty Niner was back on his proper lead, balanced and moving along nicely.

We were now in the middle of the pack, blocked behind a wall of horses and a heavy cloud of dirt. I moved him to the outside so he could see daylight, and began to push him hard. Forty Niner excelled again, and in the same move that he had made in the Kentucky Derby against Winning Colors, he charged toward the head of the pack. But it was too late. We came in fourth, beaten by a few lengths.

Everyone understood. Mr. Hancock and Woody were disappointed, but they knew that Forty Niner had run his best and that I had ridden in the best interests of their horse. After the race I approached Seth and said, "Maybe if I'd hit him with the whip after he took his first bad step, maybe he would have gone right on. . . ." "Julie," he replied, "how were you supposed to know? In the next step he could have hurt himself." The Breeders' Cup was Forty Niner's last race before going to stud, so Mr. Hancock was grateful that his bobble on the track hadn't caused a serious injury.

Before the race it was rumored that Forty Niner would be awarded an Eclipse Award if he won the Cup. Mr. Hancock was sad that Forty Niner wasn't given that award, but he knew that his horse had accomplished so many things in his career that the award would just have added one more feather to his cap. Forty Niner had a full headdress already.

I wasn't quite as philosophical. After the race I sat in the dark of the jocks' room and watched the reruns of the Cup. Eventually the screen went dark, but I continued to stare at it, listening to the voice inside my head. Had I ridden my best? Had I done anything wrong when I'd sat back on Forty Niner? I ran through the race a hundred times, but I knew that the answers weren't in my head — they were in my heart.

To ride in my first Breeders' Cup on a horse like Forty Niner for a stable like Claiborne Farm and a trainer like Woody Stephens was an overwhelming experience. I'd wanted everything to go smoothly. Not just because I was the first woman ever to ride in the Cup, but because I knew I could win. It wasn't enough to make history by being the first female. That has never been sufficient for me.

That night I packed my bag and trudged out of the jocks' room toward my hotel. In my heart I knew that I'd ridden my best. But sometimes that just doesn't feel like enough.

– 16 –

PEGASUS

"I'm a rider, too." That's what Mark O'Brien, a kid who used to hang out at the New Jersey tracks to watch races, told me. "Really?" I asked with some disbelief as my eyes scanned his leg braces and crutches. "Really," he replied. "I rode this weekend in a horse show and I got first place." I told Mark I thought that was fantastic and went off to ride my next race, still unsure about the truth of his statements.

"What's that on your shirt?" I asked Cathy Clark at a jumping show in the fall of 1989. On her shirt was an emblem of a horse with a silhouette of a person on arm crutches reaching up to pet the horse. Cathy told me that she was a member of an organization named SPUR (Special People United to Ride), which taught handicapped children how to ride horses. She explained that SPUR was begun in 1982 by a group of citizens in Monmouth County who wanted to donate some land in Huber Woods to the community. It had begun with only one horse, named Rocky, and it had since expanded into a large program with eight horses, five instructors, and more than sixty-three participants.

When I was a child, my mother gave riding lessons to a mentally handicapped girl in our community. When the lessons began, my mother would instruct the girl to walk or trot, and the child would break into hysterical laughter. But my mother never gave up, and by the end of her first summer, that little girl was riding a pony completely in control. I'll never forget the look of pride on her face as she circled the ring.

"Cathy, I don't have much time, but I want to be involved with SPUR," I said. Cathy told me that it would be very helpful if SPUR could put me on the honorary board of directors. "Put me on the *real* board," I told her. A week later I went to my first directors' meeting. I was given a tour of the facility and introduced to Pegasus, the first horse that new participants at SPUR ride. Pegasus, Peggy for short, is a wooden horse balanced on wooden peg legs. She has red and green lights on her head that light up when a child pulls the reins correctly. Then I met all the ponies and several of the kids. I was hooked.

I began to raise money at the racetrack and organized a fund-raising event where all the New York jockeys donated some of their winnings on a given day to SPUR. I pledged to match their total donation. "Please ride for people who ride but can't ride as fast as you," I implored. Every single New York jockey participated in the fund-raiser. I hadn't expected any less from them. Jockeys, as a rule, are very generous, spending a lot of their spare time at hospitals and participating in fund-raisers. The money we raised that day helped SPUR participants who came from lower income families to purchase riding equipment, and enabled SPUR to offer riding scholarships.

Children who are handicapped rarely have the chance to experience any activity that gives them a rush of adrenaline. Many days, they simply get up, bathe, and then put on their clothes. Their whole lives they hear people tell them, "You can't do this, you can't do that." Then they come to SPUR and they are no longer bound to their wheelchairs or crutches, or hindered by their minds.

Every child who rides a pony can communicate with a live, warm, responsive animal and can control their own movement, speed, and direction. Those children become mobile. They go on trail rides and see deer and rabbits. They ride up and down hills for miles and go to places they could never go in their chairs or on crutches.

Parents are amazed at the progress of their children. SPUR instructors design exercises to enhance the kids' physical abilities and to build up their confidence. There is no way to describe the happiness of parents as their child rides past them waving and calling, "See ya later, I'm going on a trail ride!"

Most of the participants at SPUR eventually leave to attend able-bodied riding programs at other barns. They have to leave, because they become so good that they need advanced instruction. And that's what makes SPUR such a special organization — it allows those kids to be equal with the rest of the world.

– 17 –

MEADOWLANDS AND MONMOUTH MEMORIES

MARY ANN ALLIGOOD told me not to do it, but on November 24, 1989, I sat in the jocks' room at Meadowlands with my calendar, marking down how many more wins I needed to reach two thousand. "Julie, that's bad luck," she warned. I ignored her, instead focusing on racetracks and projected wins.

That day I ate a turkey sandwich before my first race. Thanksgiving leftovers — delicious. Angel Cordero always warned me not to eat before a race. If I had to have emergency surgery, the doctors wouldn't operate until four hours after my last meal. I only took a few bites that day. Anyway, I thought at the time, that's just more superstitious hooey.

My three-year-old colt's name was My Rolin. As we rounded a turn heading for home, a shadow fell over the track and he propped — straightened his legs and came to a sudden halt. I flew over My Rolin's head and landed underneath him.

He trod on me a little, but just when my brain began to register that I wasn't badly hurt, another horse struck me in the left arm. The result was a break in four places, a shoulder dislocation, and a concussion.

I lay in the middle of the track on my back, my arm twisted above my head at a sickening angle, my legs thrashing the air, trying to kick away the hot licks of pain. "Krone has fallen off My Rolin, but we can see by her legs that she's definitely not paralyzed," Sam Boulmetis announced over the loudspeakers. He laughed when he said that — probably out of relief. His son was paralyzed in a riding accident.

"Get away from me!" I screamed at the veterinarian. "I'm okay, don't touch me!" The concussion had made me confused — I was certain the vet had come over to put me down because I had a broken arm. I guess I thought I was a horse. The ambulance pulled up beside me. When the paramedics tried to put an air cast on my arm, I almost fainted from the crunching and grinding of my bones. "Please don't touch my arm," I begged. Finally, I found a way to make the process less painful by pulling my mangled arm straight. I held my own arm all the way to the hospital. Things got worse when I arrived.

No one was there for me. Snake was visiting family, my friends were riding their races and taking care of their horses. It was a very eerie feeling to be hurt badly for the first time in my whole life, and to be alone. The doctor told me that I was going to have surgery, and all I could think to say was, "When will I be able to ride again?" "Ride?" he replied, "you'll be lucky if you have full use of your arm. Now, when was the last time you ate?"

Okay, so Angel Cordero was right. That's all I could think

of as I lay for an hour waiting for my turkey sandwich to digest so that I could be given painkillers and have my operation. An hour with a severely broken arm and no painkillers is too long — five minutes would be too long. John Forbes arrived and immediately took control. He and Pat McBurney, his best friend and assistant trainer in New Jersey, made sure that I was getting a good surgeon.

Right before I went into the operating room, Mary Ann showed up at the hospital. "Julie, do you want me to bring your calendar to the hospital so that after the surgery you can redo all the dates?" she joked with an evil grin. I'm probably the only person to ever enter an operating room laughing.

"What are you trying to do to me?" Snake whined when I woke up in the recovery room. "How can I make money off you if you're hurt?" I tried to smile. He sat down on the side of my bed and fixed me with his brown puppy-dog eyes. "Are you okay, Julie? Does it hurt really bad?" he asked. "Yeah, Snakey, it really hurts," I replied as I laid my head on his shoulder.

It took eight months for my arm to heal. When the doctors X-rayed it two months after the first operation, they discovered that my bone had formed a ghost bone. The inside of my bone was still solidly broken, but the outside had formed a film, or the ghost of a bone, that covered the real break. My arm had to be cut open, probed in order to find where the break was, and then rebroken. The doctors took a bone graft from my hip and put it in my arm to help the process, because once a bone stops communicating with its broken half, stops telling it to grow and reconnect, another bone has to be inserted to aid in the connection.

Recuperating from the bone graft was more painful than the initial surgery because of the force used to extract bone. For the bone graft operation, I was laid atop sandbags, the skin on my hip cut, and then bone chiseled from my hip. When I awoke, I felt heavy, nauseating pain in my left hip and the base of my spine. But the bone graft worked, and on July 25, 1990, I returned to racing and a meet at Monmouth.

I won my first race aboard a three-year-old maiden named Two Ques, trained by Willard Thompson. That race gave me my nineteen-hundredth career win and was truly a storybook comeback. I never doubted that I would ride successfully again, but after eight months off I was afraid I'd be a little rusty. Following that race I felt euphoric — I was back. I thought all my fellow jockeys were glad to have me return to the track, but I was wrong.

It took a week before I knew anything for certain. At first it was just a feeling, like when you sense a spider crawling on you before you see it, or feel someone's shadow before they come into sight. I'd handicap a race, and then horses with characteristic running styles would run differently and in a way that always messed up my horse's running style. If I had a horse with speed and there weren't any other horses in the race with the same type of speed, another jockey would push his horse to run faster, not to win the race, but just to tire out my horse with a speed battle. If I was on the outside, a jockey would make his horse run wide, so that I'd get fanned out and my horse's energy would be drained from traveling the track in such a wide trip.

I began to notice that wherever I was, first, third, or even fifth, there was always another rider matching my style. No matter where I was riding, I'd hear jockeys yell over to each other, "She's on the inside, move over," or "Watch it, she's coming up." It happened too often to ignore. I'd move up to surge through a hole, and I'd watch the hole shut in a split-second and find myself dangerously close to the rail. "No, no, no! Don't do it!" I'd scream at whatever jockey was squeezing me that race. But he'd just make my trip tighter. Those jockeys' actions threatened both my welfare and my horses'. Seven days after I returned to Monmouth, I stood in the jocks' shower and cried.

I finally confided in John Forbes. "John, there is a group of jockeys that are ganging up on me during races. It's driving me crazy and it's dangerous. What should I do?" John was surprised by who the particular jockeys were, but after several more days of watching the races, he realized that what I had told him was true and called me into his office to talk. "You can't confront them, Julie," John advised. "It will only make them stronger if they know how much they're getting to you. And if other trainers and owners find out what's going on, they're not going to want to ride you, because they'll figure they won't win." I felt trapped. "Learn from it, Julie," John urged. "If you can, outwit them at their own game, and in the process you'll become a better rider." So that's what I did.

If I had a horse with known speed who was in front his whole life, I'd break from the gate slowly, put my hands down, and pull my horse back. Then I'd ride nice and easy on the outside in third or fourth. The group of jockeys that were after me would be pushing hard on their horses' necks, trying to stay forward to inhibit my horse. I'd watch them stand up and look around. Hey, where's Krone, they'd wonder. Then I'd slide to the front and beat them all. I developed a knack for making horses race opposite to their form.

I didn't just beat them. One by one, I talked to them. "Hey, why are you doing this to me?" I'd ask sincerely. I discovered that there was one strong leader in the group. He was an older jockey with a bitter edge, who obviously harbored some sort of jealousy of me. I was young, and before my accident more successful than he'd ever been. I never ended up confronting that jockey, but the rest of the group slowly began to leave me alone. By then, though, it didn't matter. I had followed John's advice, and I had become a better rider. Good enough to outwit them at their shameful game.

Today that same nasty jockey is still part of the racetrack. He's trying to move up in the establishment's ranks, to be a steward or a Jockeys' Guild official. My stomach turns when I see him, and he is fake and nice to me. But I no longer feel the need to name him or show his real nature to the world. I know his true colors, and he has to live with himself. That's enough.

The Monmouth meet concluded on Labor Day, 1990. I ended up the fourth-leading rider at the meet, and in the end I was proud of my place. I'd worked my butt off to come in fourth.

It was time to move on to the September through December meet at Meadowlands. However, in the back of my mind I was beginning to consider some additional advice that John Forbes had given me. "Go to New York," he'd said. "You're ready for the big time." I knew he was right. But while I'd ridden several races at New York tracks, my experiences had always sent me running back to New Jersey, where I had ridden longer and felt more comfortable.

– 18 –

TRULY HOME

STEWARD SAM BOULMETIS once said that a spill from a horse is similar to a giant wave hitting you while swimming in the ocean. When it hits, you think Oh, no, and hold your breath while spinning beneath the surface. Sometimes the water forces you to the bottom and you get sand burns. Sometimes it bounces you around, and when you're finally washed onto the beach, there's sand in your pants, your neck is twisted, and there's a bump on your head. Every wave is different. So is every spill.

The only thing that every spill has in common is that whatever the physical result, it is far outweighed by the mental anguish. A jockey simply cannot fall during a race and not suffer some sort of wound to her confidence. Nearly thirteen out of every one thousand jockeys are killed in spills — the highest mortality rate of any sport. Racing averages twenty-five hundred injuries and two deaths per year. No matter how experienced or talented a jockey is, those statistics are frightening. During 1988, I fell off three times at New York racetracks.

On April 24, 1988, I went down in the stretch at Aqueduct racetrack in South Ozone Park, New York. I was riding a filly named Rouge for trainer Bobby Klesaris. We were in the lead the whole race, but in the stretch Rouge began to diminish (noticeably slow). I lost my position and dropped back to the rail while other horses began to pass me. Robby Davis took the lead, with Randy Romero moving up on a horse that was quicker than both mine and Davis's. In order for Romero to clear Davis's heels or go around his horse, he had to move to the rail. As Romero made his move, Davis drifted in a bit, and when Romero went by me on the outside and dropped in front of me on the rail, there was no longer enough space for my horse. I stood up on Rouge to steady her back so that her legs wouldn't cross with Romero's horse. Rouge stumbled and I pulled on the reins hard and was immediately shot over her head.

I held onto Rouge's neck for a few strides and then lost my grip and dropped right in front of her. Imagine hanging onto a horse's neck when it is running full blast and then just letting go right in front of its body. Rouge ran right over me, striking me under my left arm so hard that the main nerve was damaged and I couldn't move my hand or fingers for some time. My chin was badly cut, and my shoulder was loosened in its socket. I was lucky.

Two weeks later I was riding a horse for Bobby Klesaris that had just been vetted — checked by the vet for soundness using ultrasound techniques. He was a beautiful little chestnut horse who looked like a miniature Secretariat. We won our race by so much that I began to ease up on him in the stretch instead of after the wire. A few strides after the wire, my horse fell. It was unbelievable — he had just been vetted, had just easily won a race, and then had broken his leg three strides after the wire. I was bruised but uninjured. The horse had to be put down.

Finally, there was a spill on Labor Day at Belmont Park that left me so shell-shocked that I was certain that New York was not the place for me. Richie Migliore and Chris Antley were riding close in the stretch. Chris's horse bumped Pat Day's horse's rear end, which forced her legs to cross. She fell in the stretch, and Chris went right over her head. Richie couldn't avoid Chris's horse, which lay sideways on the track, and his horse ran straight into her. Richie was catapulted over the horse and landed on his neck and face. Meanwhile, Chris's horse was rotated toward the rail by the blow. I had moved to the inside to avoid Chris and Richie, and now Chris's horse was directly in my path. His horse tried to rise in front of me, and when my horse hit her, I was sent sailing into the rail. I struck the plastic full force with my entire backside.

It all happened in mere seconds. As we lay on the turf, I turned my head to see how Richie and Chris were. Richie's face was a bloody mess, and there was grass sticking out of his mouth. He was barely conscious. Chris lay a bit farther from me, unconscious from the blow to his head. I felt like we had been in a battle, and now I lay on the ground with my best friends bleeding and broken beside me.

We all survived. Richie's neck was broken, and he spent months in the hospital and endured several operations, including the temporary removal of his voice box, the fusion of vertebrae, and the pain of wearing a halo brace. Throughout the ordeal, his only question was When can I ride again? Eventually, Richie Migliore did ride again.

For five days, Chris Antley thought he was in school, not the hospital. He had a severe concussion, but after a week he came back to reality. And a few years later Chris won the Kentucky Derby. He, too, never considered giving up riding. I came out of the spill with the fewest difficulties. My back and legs were terribly bruised, and at first I couldn't walk. It took several weeks before I was fit to ride again, but I, too, never considered quitting.

There's a song by Willie Nelson called "Still Is Still Moving to Me," about the Air Force's crack pilots, the Blue Angels. The words say, "I don't know how to put into words how to feel, but I know that it's real, and still is still moving to me." Whenever I hear that song I wonder what makes a pilot like a Blue Angel want to fly. The close maneuvers they perform as a team leave no room for error — if they make a mistake they run a very high risk of dying. I've read that when a Blue Angel does survive a near-death experience, he's up flying the next day. It's like horse racing. There is a discipline, a narrow margin for error, and an intensity that translates into an unbelievably rewarding experience.

When I watch the Blue Angels I think, Those guys are nuts. But at the same time, I know that can be said about jockeys, too. I've made up a saying about the racetrack: You just ride 'til you fall off and then you ride 'til you fall off and then you ride 'til you fall off. . . . I guess that's as true as Willy's song.

After my three accidents, I did become gun-shy of New

York racetracks. It's hard not to harbor some superstitions when you're a jockey. I returned to New Jersey, but I no longer felt truly comfortable there. I had had too many negative experiences with jockeys there after my 1989 broken arm at Meadowlands. I knew that it was time to go someplace new. I decided that after the fall meet in New Jersey, I would once again try New York.

I was winning the Monmouth meet when I had my next accident. Bobby Klesaris had asked me to gallop a horse for him. While jockeys don't usually gallop horses, it's not a big deal to help out when a trainer needs a rider. I hopped on Bobby's baby and galloped her. As I passed the stands where Bobby, John Forbes, and several other trainers sat watching their horses gallop, my horse bucked. I went over her head and landed on my feet, the reins still in my hand. I landed wrong, and heard the bones in my ankle snap before I felt the pain and crumpled to the ground. "Hey, I just broke my ankle," I yelled over to John. "You did not," he called back. "Just get up." I said, "John, I'm serious, it's really broken." He ran for the ambulance. By then, Snake was at my side.

The ambulance wouldn't go to the hospital where my friend Dr. Angelo Chinnici worked, so Snake drove me. He ran every red light from the track to the hospital, and there must have been twenty-five of them. Snake is a terrible driver under any conditions, but that day he got me to the hospital without an accident or being stopped by the cops. When we arrived, I sent him to get me some coffee and a donut while I got my X rays.

When Angelo stopped in to look at my X rays, he informed me that it didn't look too bad. He was just trying to make me feel better. My ankle bone was broken in three places. By the time Snake returned, I was already in the cast room. "What do you mean she's in the cast room?" Snake yelled at a nurse. The nurse told him I was getting a cast on my ankle. "No, she's not!" he shouted. I could hear Snake grumbling to himself in the hallway before he came into the room and gave me a big hug.

I went to Nantucket to spend a few days resting on the beach. Snake called to tell me that there was a rider who was only ten winners behind me for leading rider. The call made me feel sick, because I knew there was enough time before the end of the meet for that rider to pass me. Four days after I arrived on Nantucket, I soaked my cast off, went to the doctor, and had an air cast made to fit into my boot. Then I returned to Monmouth Park. When the 1990 meet ended, I was still the leading rider, broken ankle and all. It was a good way to start my New York career.

I was also ready to make some changes in my life. I was tired of renting apartments, living with roommates, never having a home. Having my own house was one of my biggest childhood fantasies. To own a house and farm, to have paid for it on my own, was a dream. The fact that the dream came true is at times overwhelming.

In 1990 I purchased a farm in New Jersey. I have never regretted it. It's not just the location, fields, country air, or quiet, but the warmth I feel when I'm at home. My house, weathered wood and brick, isn't really big, although it's a lot bigger on the inside than it looks on the outside. I've filled it with comfortable furniture, some antiques, and soft rugs that make everyone who visits feel at home.

At the time I bought the farm, I wasn't certain that I would always be a New York rider, but I decided that if I did race predominantly in New York, the commute wouldn't be too terrible. I had fallen in love with the place and knew that regardless of where I rode, I had to buy it. I named my farm Jockey Hollow.

A stone's throw from my house, right out the back door, are green paddocks and a large wooden barn connected to an indoor riding arena. The barn has nineteen stalls, which house fifteen other horses as well as my own, Peter Rabbit and Chicago. Peter Rabbit is the horse my mother bred for me from It'saGrayIssue. He has just as much grit and determination as he had when my mother was training him in Florida. And just as his spirit helped my mom to fight her cancer, it helps take my mind off the pressures of my job. Chicago is a twelve-year-old ex-racehorse, a little bay thoroughbred with a few flecks of white on his face. I've had him for two years, and he is still a bit high strung and neurotic. He isn't fond of small places like trailers, and gets nervous if he's held too tight. I learned to jump fences on Chicago. He allowed me to make mistakes, and he fixed them so we could jump properly and get around a course. Chicago's potential as a jumper is limited compared to the younger Peter, but he does his job well.

Charlotte Koziarz is my barn manager. She is my peace of mind, my friend and confidante, and one of the most knowledgeable horse-persons I've ever known. Charlotte's husband is a racehorse trainer in New Jersey, but Charlotte prefers working with show horses, jumpers, and dressage horses. One of Charlotte's most valuable characteristics is that she never leaves bases open. If a horse has any type of problem, Charlotte not only notices, but knows how to solve it. She remembers when each horse needs to be wormed, shoed, and exercised, and constantly monitors their diets. My barn at home is my hobby, but for Charlotte it is a number-one priority.

Not just horses, but animals in general have always been a special part of my life. I have two cats, Snigglefritz and Kunta Kitty, that live in my house. Having animals around makes the house even warmer — there's nothing so good for the inside of a person as the outside of an animal.

I have always tried to place myself in an environment that feels safe and secure, and that reminds me of the best parts of my childhood. Sometimes I sit on the porch of my home and watch the morning sunlight glance off the horses that play in the paddocks. I smell the crisp, sweet air and listen to whinnies and nickers. For a moment I'm a child again, perched on the steps of my parents' farmhouse in Eau Claire. I wonder where Filly and I will spend our day playing — maybe we'll find a new trail and race through tunnels of orange and yellow autumn leaves. I can hear them crunch beneath my pony's hooves. And later, as I drive down the interstate to the racetrack, I can still feel the wind brushing our faces, beckoning us to adventure.

− 19 −

RIDING THE BIG APPLE

Hey, that's Angel Cordero riding beside me, his arms flailing, silks brushing against mine. That's all I could think my first few months as a New York rider. I was in the major leagues. New York riders include most of the top riders in the country, with the remainder riding in California at Hollywood Park, Del Mar, and Santa Anita. The reason that the top jockeys go to New York and California is simple — that's where the biggest owners, best horses, and largest purses are. Consequently, when jockeys ride successfully in New York and California, they earn both their reputations and more money. Reputations and large purses can also be won at Gulfstream Park in Florida when New York jockeys move down there during the winter months to race in warmer weather.

When I first began riding in New York, I just wanted to stop in the middle of the race and take it all in. I was riding with legends — Angel Cordero, Jorge Velasquez, José Santos.

These were the riders who won the Triple Crown (the Kentucky Derby, the Preakness Stakes, and the Belmont Stakes), and most of the stakes races (races for bigger purses than the typical daily race, where the owner usually pays a fee to run his horse, and to which the track adds more money to make the total purse). These were the jockeys whose photos had hung on my bedroom wall — the stuff of my dreams.

In the beginning, just moving into the starting gate with jockeys like that was overwhelming. When the novelty wore off, I realized that I needed to rise to their level in order to compete successfully with them. So I didn't just ride with those jockeys, I learned from them.

I was no longer catching glimpses of the superstars, but racing with them every day. In the past, I'd seen riders like Angel Cordero only for one race when he visited New Jersey, or when I rode one in New York. Now I had the opportunity to spend time with him, to study and learn from his style. It was Angel who told me to move my stirrups into a position that helped me to become a more steady rider. Just as it was Angel who during a race hit me with his whip and taught me a valuable lesson.

"You hit me in the arm with your whip and look how swollen and red it is," I complained to Angel after he whacked me in the stretch and then beat me by a nose. Angel sincerely replied, "Well, Julie, I guess you were riding too close then." I walked away thinking, I must have been too close. As I entered the jocks' room, I stopped in my tracks. What was he talking about, "too close"? Angel had hit me in the arm so that I couldn't push my horse well, and then he'd beaten me. I'd been had. But I wasn't angry, I had learned something about being a smart rider. And the next time I had the opportunity, I did it to someone else in the stretch. When that jockey confronted me, I said, "Sorry, I guess you must have been too close."

Riding in New York became an exciting challenge. Races set up differently there. Riders box each other in tighter, and timing becomes split second. At the same time, there is no maliciousness or stupidity, just aggressiveness in the heat of the battle. And there's a camaraderie in New York racing that I never experienced in New Jersey. The New York jockeys are extremely professional. And having already proven they're a success, they have such confidence in their abilities that once the battle is over, it's over.

During my first meet in Atlantic City, I had seen the helicopters bring Angel Cordero and Jorge Velasquez to the big stakes races. I had watched them ride the horses I usually rode, and instead of being bent out of shape I'd thought Let me be as good as they are. At the same time, Chris Antley had been sitting on a bale of hay pretending he was a jockey in a race and thinking, I wish I could get the chance to ride. . . . Maybe someday I'll be as successful as Julie Krone. In 1990 we had come full circle. I was beginning to have successes in New York against riders like Cordero and Santos. Chris's career had accelerated after he began to ride in Atlantic City, and he, too, had moved to New York. Chris and I were once again riding together, this time as equals — two country kids who had had a dream and made it happen. Several months later, another one of my dreams came true.

In 1990 I was invited to attend an international jockeys' competition in Tokyo. My New York riding career had just begun, and while I had generated interest among several train-ers, Snake and I felt that taking the trip wouldn't hurt my racing career, because I wouldn't be gone long enough for the trainers to forget me. No one told me that I would be the first woman ever to ride at the Tokyo racetrack, or that the crowd attending the competition would number approximately 170,000 fans. But things couldn't have been handled more perfectly, includ-ing the construction of a makeshift female jockeys' room just for me. The Japanese were extremely well organized through-out the competition. It was a joy to ride in Tokyo, because nothing went wrong. And they treated all the jockeys with so much respect and kindness that we felt like royalty.

Riding in Japan is very different from riding in America. First, some of the courses run to the right rather than to the left. To a jockey, the switch in direction feels like driving on the wrong side of the road. Second, there is a longer warm-up with the pony people (riders who accompany racers as they warm up their horses and lead them to the starting gate), which gives jockeys much more time to assess their horses and how they are moving and feeling.

I didn't worry about any of the differences in Tokyo. I was thrilled to have been invited to the competition and to have the opportunity to race beneath the glory of Mount Fuji against jockeys from all over the world. In particular, I was excited to race with my childhood hero, Steve Cauthen, "The Kid."

On the first day of races at the Tokyo racetrack, my valet took me to the main locker room to see where my tack was being stored. It is hard to describe the feelings I had when I saw Steve Cauthen's name inscribed on the box right next to my own. My father had traveled to Japan with me, and I turned to him and said, "Dad, can you believe this? Is this too incredible?" It is truly overwhelming when a dream comes true. Then Steve walked into the locker room.

"Steve," I sputtered, "my name is Julie Krone, and you're one of the reasons I decided to become a jockey." I felt so stupid. He must have heard that line from thousands of kids just like me. But Steve didn't make me feel at all uncomfortable. He was even more gracious and kind than he appeared on television or in his book. Throughout the following week, I spent hours talking to Steve about being a jockey. I asked him how I should handle publicity when it became overwhelming, how to handle losses graciously, and how to speak intelligently to the media. Steve's answers were simple and made a lot of sense. I took everything he told me to heart. And finally the day came when we were no longer just talking but racing side by side.

Saturday, November 24, 1990, at the Tokyo racetrack I rode in a three-year-old-and-up eighteen-hundred-meter (eleven eighths of a mile) international jockeys' turf race (a race on grass) with Steve Cauthen. I was representing the United States, Steve, England, and the rest of the jockeys, Ireland, Sweden, and a host of other countries that were their homelands. My horse's name was Cyber Field, and we were a bit of a long shot in the race because he had never before run this distance. We moved out of the gate slowly, but after I sat quietly on him for a moment, Cyber Field literally began to drag me to the lead, grabbing the thick green turf and pulling it toward him with amazing power. He had the longest stride I have ever seen, and we flowed over the course, glistening black muscles and a tightly wound rider. Cyber Field just kept going faster and faster. Oh, no, I thought, is he going to get tired by the time we reach the stretch? In the stretch Steve tried to make a run at me. I pushed on Cyber Field's neck and asked him to run, and he took off faster than any other horse I had ever ridden. We put Steve away.

To slow after the wire aboard a magnificent horse, beneath Mount Fuji and the thundering cheers of fans who had never seen a woman win at their racetrack, was unbelievable. I walked back to the jockeys' room in shock. "Dad, this is so amazing," I said. "I used to dream of riding like Steve Cauthen, and hoped that someday I might be a jockey, and now here I am, in Japan, racing with my hero." "Yeah," Steve began as he walked up behind me, "she used to dream about being a jockey, and about someday meeting me, and now she comes to Tokyo and kicks my butt!" I turned around and he was smiling at me. "Steve," I replied, meeting his smile with one of my own, "that was part of the dream, too."

– 20 –

TRAINERS

THE HORSE was not moving well, and he was scaring me. That's what I told Pat McBurney one summer day in 1990 after trotting his horse around the track for a mile to get him warmed up for his morning workout. Earlier in the week another jockey had scratched the horse from a race because he didn't feel comfortable with the way he was traveling. The racetrack veterinarian was standing next to Pat as I rode up, waiting to check the horse. He needed to draw blood to make sure he wasn't chemically treated with anything to make him seem sound, a standard check made on all racehorses.

When I'm on a horse for John Forbes, the vet knows that there's no question that either John or I would work a horse that wasn't sound. I've ridden John's horses for eight years, and I've only had one break down, and he just popped his shoulder out. John's in the claiming business (a licensed person can purchase a horse entered in a designated race for a predetermined price), and consequently he must have the skill not only to pur-chase sound horses, but to maintain their soundness in order to uphold the quality of his stable. To have only one of the thou-sands of horses John has claimed and I've ridden ever have a problem shows the care that John and his staff give their horses.

After the vet made a perfunctory check, I said to Pat, "This horse is traveling horribly, and he's scaring me. I don't trust him, but if you tell me to breeze him, I will." "Krone," Pat said, "breeze the horse." I did, and he breezed (raced a short dis-tance) fine. We didn't win that day, but a few days later he won a race, and he continued winning more races after that.

John Forbes and Pat McBurney taught me to trust their opinions and their concern for both my welfare and that of their horses. Pat would never have told me to breeze his horse if he wasn't positive that I wouldn't be in danger. Had he been wrong, I could have been seriously injured or killed. That's how much trust I have in him.

John Forbes's stable is a team, and that team works to-gether for a horse's well-being and for the success of the stable. It's a long process that starts the moment the groom enters a horse's stall, and it differs with every horse in the stable. The groom treats the horse a certain way according to that horse's personality. The pony girl or boy has to do certain things with him in the morning. For example, if a pony girl is leading a horse and rider to the starting gate, and she knows that the horse hates to be pushed or impeded in any way before a race, she has to work correctly with him to make sure that he is in the best possible frame of mind before the race. John feeds each horse different foods. Pat then puts each on an individual gal-loping schedule, and I breeze them each a certain way. Every one of us observes the horse, and then the trainer makes adjustments to the horse's schedule based on our recommendations. What separates a good trainer from a mediocre one is attention to small details.

John taught me that when I get off a horse after a race, I should be completely honest with the trainer. Pointing out every problem after the race — the quality of the track, my horse's weaknesses, other jockeys — and not analyzing my own performance, doesn't help John train his horse, or me to win on him. If I mess up, then that's what I have to tell John, because I'm part of a team. A trainer has to know if his horse didn't race to his ability because of a mistake I made or because he got boxed in. And a trainer has to have faith in his jockey's opinions as well as her abilities.

John Forbes was the first trainer I ever worked for who let me be me. When I would try things with his horses that were out of the ordinary, things like taking a horse away from the pony person during the post parade (when horses are ridden from the paddock to the starting gate past the stands), he'd watch me without a word. Most jockeys stay with their pony person in order to calm their horse or make him comfortable before a race, but I try to be extremely sensitive to what the horse I'm riding needs, and to meet those needs. There have been times when I've left my pony girl or walked one of John's horses in the post parade as opposed to warming him up by trotting and galloping to loosen his muscles and relax him, and other times I've breezed his horse slowly. Every time I do something different, John just says, "Krone, that's a little bit weird, but if it works for you, then do it." He has always trusted my horse sense, my intuition, and my abilities. And when the things I've tried work, he says, "Good job, Julie, that was really different, but it worked well with that horse."

Unfortunately, John Forbes's operation is based in New Jersey, and with his prodding, in 1990 I had finally made the decision to become a New York rider. That meant developing relationships with new trainers.

If there is a New York version of John Forbes, it's Pete Ferriola. Pete has a predominant claiming stable, and was among the first trainers in New York to ride me. Pete's most impressive quality as a trainer, besides his ability to claim well, is the philosophy he applies to his horses. Pete doesn't believe in squeezing all the juice out of the lemon and then sending the rind down the road. He claims horses, and a few weeks later has them winning stakes races. Then he runs them until they're nine years old, steadily moving them up the ladder of success. That way, his horses stay a solid level above the price he claimed them for, and his stable remains powerful.

It is understandable that I tried to develop relationships with trainers in New York who had some of the qualities that I value in John Forbes. Allen Jerkens is a wonderful New York trainer who also believes that a jockey should be herself. He says that there is a point in certain jockeys' careers when they give up being automatically generic in their riding. And at that point they become great riders. But he understands that there is a risk involved in doing things differently. It's great when a rider accomplishes something by trying new moves, but at the same time that jockey puts her butt on the line. If she messes up, she looks worse than if she had just ridden generically. There is a point where I risk looking stupid in order to do something that comes naturally to me, something that's different but makes my horse work, run, and produce. For that reason, Allen began to ride me.

Allen Jerkens trains his horses differently from other trainers, and makes that difference work. He's part horse. He hangs out at his barn all day long, never leaves, just sits there watching the horses and wondering what they're thinking. I can tell Allen whatever I think about a horse, and he won't look at me like I'm from outer space. We're in touch with the nature of horses, and we share our insights. And, it's because of Allen's ability to understand his animals that his style as a trainer is, at times, peculiar to outsiders. For example, he'll breeze his horses from the wire to the half-mile pole when the opposite is the norm. He lets some of his horses eat hay right up to race time. Horses are like runners, usually they don't perform well if they eat right before a race. But to Allen every horse is an individual, with individual needs. Sometimes Allen feeds his horses by hand. But the bottom line is that he finds out what works, regardless of conventionality.

Great trainers give jockeys the opportunity to be great. When I became a New York rider, Bill Mott was the first trainer to put me on a steady group of stakes horses (horses who compete primarily in stakes races and consequently have the opportunity to win big purses). Jockeys usually want to stay at New York meets on the weekends because their Saturday and Sunday mounts are strong. When I first went to New York, my weekend mounts were not the leading contenders in any race. For that reason, when Bill Mott asked me to travel on the weekends to different racetracks, where stakes races were being run at the same time as New York's races, I agreed.

It was a wonderful opportunity for me; I wasn't giving up

much, and I was getting to win big stakes races for a prominent trainer. And the chance to sit on an impressive stable of blue-blooded horses was a valuable education. Riding for Bill taught me to recognize greatness in a wide variety of horses, to understand that greatness comes in all different styles — nervous, calm, big, small, sprinting, long running, and those that prefer turf courses to dirt ones. Each of Bill's horses is bred for a different kind of excellence, and I began to recognize that and ride accordingly.

Bill Mott is a wonderful trainer, not only because of his knowledge and expertise. It doesn't matter if Bill has seventy horses in training or if he is at times the leading trainer in the world, he still shows up at the barn every morning at six A.M. He works all day, never sits back or lets one small detail slip by. He holds that if a trainer is doing well, that's all the more reason to work hard. That ethic can be seen in every hot-walker, exercise rider, groom, foreman, and jockey who works for him. Bill has a wonderful way of communicating and gets the most out of everyone.

When I first moved to New York, Scotty Schulhofer kept me on my tiptoes. I was afraid of him. Scotty and his son, Randy, who is also a trainer, have an extremely powerful stable, and the chance to ride for them was a golden opportunity. I knew that Scotty wasn't keen on girl jockeys, so the first time I came into his barn I was just hoping for a chance to ride for him. But it took a while before I worked up the courage to talk to Scotty. His foreman, Sal, would tell me to ask him if I could gallop or breeze a horse for him. I wouldn't, because I didn't know what to say, and I was afraid to say something wrong. Still, I hung around like an eager puppy, nervous but hoping to be noticed.

Two weeks later I began to ride some of Scotty's horses that traveled funny or were a bit slow. I jumped at the chance, just for the momentary opportunity to hang on the shirt tails of his success. I'd ride those horses with all my heart and soul, and usually end up third or fourth. Sal would point out to Scotty that I'd tried really hard, but it wasn't until I won my first race for him that Scotty began to notice me. The horse I won on was named Fun, Fun, Fun. I ran around the shed row after the race, smiling and chanting, "Fun, Fun, Fun." Scotty started to let me ride out-of-town stakes races, and soon I was one of his main jockeys.

Scotty and Randy taught me a lot about training and about how a stable becomes powerful. To understand that is to understand not only the talent of the trainers but also their ability to produce tangible results. Trainers who have a stable of horses that win attract owners who have both the money to purchase quality horses and the savvy to know that a great horse can only be great with the proper training. Some owners have their own farms for breeding and training, but many turn to trainers like Scotty and Randy to mold their horses into winners.

In addition to the knowledge I gained from working with the Schulhofers, there was one particularly valuable lesson Scotty shared that helped me win the biggest race of my life. There are a lot of horses with split personalities, and as Scotty trains a horse that personality changes, progresses from day to day. There are times when the same horse can be aloof one race and aggressive the next. Scotty taught me not to expect anything but instead to adjust. And he gave me the chance to ride difficult, talented athletes, which in turn allowed me great success.

A great trainer and wonderful racehorses can make a jockey an all-around rider instead of a specialized one who can win only with a certain type of horse on a particular track. Barclay Tagg and Jonathan Sheppard are trainers of that kind. Both are famous for European horses bred with a lot of depth to run on turf courses. I learned about European breeding and temperament from Jonathan and Barclay. They also taught me how to ride in a European style to get the most out of that type of horse.

European jockeys hit their horses a bit less than American riders. They also tend to keep their horses more covered up (behind other horses instead of racing out in the clear) and ride with their reins longer to get their horses off the bridles, allowing more range of motion. If I rode one of Barclay's or Jonathan's horses in a more controlling American style, he would probably not race to his full potential. The horse would think, Why did my trainer put this jockey on my back? She doesn't understand my style.

Working for trainers who understand different styles and have different goals makes a jockey a well-rounded athlete. John Forbes has taught me the science behind how to recognize potential and evaluate the probability of future successes. Jonathan and Barclay have taught me how to ride European distance turf horses, and Billy Mott has given me the ability to rate the potential of a horse against other horses racing in a stakes race. It's not just riding blue-blooded horses that brings success, but riding many kinds, and showing a trainer that you're willing to struggle to learn for them and are determined to win every race possible.

— 21 —

SAINT BALLADO'S STORY

RACE RIDING ISN'T just about riding for Billy Mott, Scotty Schulhofer, Allen Jerkens, or John Forbes. It's about taking the time to ride for trainers of smaller stables as well, the guys who work just as hard and sometimes have their whole career hinging on a single horse. When a jockey first begins her career, she focuses on riding for the big names, because that's how her own name will grow. There is a certain degree of pressure in riding for powerful barns; they can make or break a jockey. I learned later in my career, however, that there is a great sense of personal responsibility when riding for a small barn. Those trainers don't just want you to win, they *need* you to win.

Racing can be very much equated to the movie industry. The owners are the producers, the trainers are the directors, the jockeys are the actors, and the horses are the script. Trainers and jockeys must have a level of communication that borders on the extrasensory in order to make the performance of a horse successful. A trainer can spend months preparing a horse for a campaign only to see his work flushed down the toilet by a jockey's inaction, lack of consideration, confusion, lack of interest, or mistakes.

Choosing the right jockey for a horse is a very important decision, especially for lesser-known trainers who have only one or two good horses in their barn and need those horses to win, both to make enough money to sustain their operation and to draw in more owners. Not all jockeys are right for every situation. There are jockeys who are movie stars in the racing industry. They are excellent riders but can lose their perspective because of fame, fortune, and performance pressures. There are jockeys who are solid actors, professionals who perform well but without flair.

In 1991, trainer Clint Goodrich was looking for a jockey who was both an actor and a movie star. He needed the whole picture in one performer. Clint's entire career was riding on a horse named Saint Ballado, whom he had purchased after his original barn, Tartan Farms, had decided to close shop and leave him without horses or financing. Saint Ballado was a full brother to two champions. He was an immature horse, not yet three years old, but had the potential to put Clint on the map and revitalize his career. If Saint Ballado didn't perform to the best of his abilities, Clint would be sunk. For all these reasons, Clint sought me out to ride his horse.

"Julie, my name is Clint Goodrich, and I have a horse I'd like you to ride." I was standing next to the blacksmith, shooting the breeze and playing with a little yellow puppy. When I shook Clint's hand and looked into his eyes, he met my gaze with a powerful intensity. This guy means business, I thought. "Well, Snake is my agent," I began, and Clint said, "Why don't the two of you come by my barn in the next few days." I agreed.

The following morning Snake and I met Clint in his barn after he returned from galloping Saint Ballado on the track. He seemed surprised to see us, and I quickly leapt to my feet from the sand where I'd been playing and moved to shake his hand. "Julie, this is the horse I'd like you to ride," Clint said. I moved over to Saint Ballado and let him bite the back of my hand. Later Clint would tell me that he could actually see all my systems turn on, the lights begin to blink, and my personality become illuminated. At the time, I was just being myself, getting to know the horse as well as the trainer.

The first time I worked Saint Ballado he was extremely quirky. As we walked back to the barn, I told Clint the things I felt he should work on with his horse. "You're saying stuff to me that I've never heard anybody communicate about my horse," Clint said in a surprised voice. Right then, he knew he'd made the choice of jockey for his horse. Our communication was on the spiritual, intuitive, insightful level that was simply a part of the way I rode. Clint just hadn't worked with a jockey like me before.

Two weeks before Saint Ballado's first big race, Snake agreed that I would ride him. Clint had invested all his own money as well as some partners' finances in Saint Ballado, and that first race was an event which would determine if he would die. One day before the race Bill Mott asked Snake to have me ride one of his horses in the same race as Clint's. Snake agreed, spinning (dropping) Clint Goodrich and Saint

Ballado. As we pulled up to Clint's barn in our golf cart, I knew that he wouldn't take the news well. But I am one of Bill Mott's and Scotty Schulhofer's main riders and have a responsibility to them to ride their horses whenever they ask. They put me on winners, and in the end, winning is the name of the game.

"The hell with Billy Mott!" Clint yelled at Snake after receiving the news. I could hear his reaction from across the barn where I stood petting Saint Ballado. "We've got to ride Mott's horse; we ride everything for Mott in New York," Snake tried to explain. "Snake, this is the best horse in my barn. He's incredibly important to me, and if I'd known you were going to spin me, I would have gotten another jockey to work with him for the last month," Clint said. "What can we do?" I said as I walked up behind Clint. "It's Billy Mott." "Julie, that just doesn't fly with me right now," Clint said and walked away. I felt terrible about the whole situation, but my hands were tied. In the end Clint used another jockey for the race. Not a bad jockey, but not a name rider.

In the paddock before the race I mouthed good luck to Clint as I passed him aboard Bill's horse Don't Sell the Farm. Clint looked nervous. It was only a ten-horse field, and each of those ten were magnificent, well-bred horses. When the starting gate clanged open, I moved out quickly, and at the top of the stretch inherited the lead from Connecticut. Saint Ballado was in third, about three off the pace on the outside. By the eighth pole I was in the lead with Saint Ballado second. The last seventy yards Saint Ballado began to pull at the turf every step of the way. We crossed the wire together, too close to call, according to the announcer. I rode back to Bill Mott, and together we waited to hear the results. Saint Ballado won by a nose.

The next morning I went to Clint's barn and congratulated him. "I'm really happy for you," I said. He held up his hands in a cross and motioned for me to get back. "Please don't be that way, Clint. I get to win a lot of races, and you don't get that many, so I'm glad you won. And, if you still want me to, I'd like to ride your horse in his next race." Clint said no, that he couldn't do that to the jockey who'd won the race for him. I understood, but in my heart I knew that I'd ride that horse again.

Several weeks later Clint called Snake and asked us to come by his barn. He was unhappy with how his jockey was riding Saint Ballado. He wanted me back. Although Saint Ballado had proved himself one time, Clint still needed him to perform well. He knew that I understood his horse and that I would bust my butt to win for him. I knew Clint's financial situation by that time, and although that put a lot of pressure on me, I wanted to win as much as he did. I began once again to breeze his horse, readying him for the Jim Beam, a prep race for the Kentucky Derby worth $500,000. At this point people were beginning to notice Clint's horse and to believe he might be a Derby contender. Things were looking up for Clint.

We lost the Jim Beam. I was sixth into the first turn, fifth up the backside and then third at the three-eighths pole. We had a great chance. There were two horses in front of me and they began to slow. I was forced to go to the outside. There is a cardinal rule in race riding: Never go inside one or around two. I went around, and the outside horse bore out badly on the turn and I was carried wide. The entire field swept by me. If that horse hadn't lugged out, Saint Ballado and I would probably have won the Beam. Clint was very disappointed and I felt terrible, but we both knew that it was the only move I could have made to win the race.

Snake decided I shouldn't ride Saint Ballado in his next race. In his next few races he didn't place in the top three. Saint Ballado was tired. He needed time to recover, and Clint was forced to withdraw him from the Kentucky Derby. A lot of people would have run that horse in the Derby anyway, but Clint loved Saint Ballado and didn't want to risk injuring him. After several months of rest and light training for his horse, Clint asked Snake if I'd ride Saint Ballado in the Arlington Classic. Snake agreed.

Saint Ballado and I ended up winning the Classic in stakes record time. When we slowed after the wire and rode over to Clint, there were tears in his eyes. Not just because he'd been right about his horse, and not just because Saint Ballado's performance would enable him to continue his career as a trainer. Those tears were the result of seeing his hard work pay off in a beautiful ride, a perfect partnership of horse and jockey. It was a confirmation of all of our abilities.

Saint Ballado ran one more time before he was put out to stud. He has a new career now as a stallion, and Clint Goodrich continues to rise in the ranks of trainers. I played a part in the success of both, which gave me as much satisfaction as riding for the big stables. And while I have a responsibility to the people who put me on their winners, I will always continue to find time to ride for lesser-known stables and trainers.

– 22 –

A HORSE IS A HORSE

"A HORSE IS a horse, of course." I don't know who said that, but they were wrong. I've ridden 15,970 horses in my career, and no two of them were alike. I don't remember them all, but there have certainly been a few that have not only helped me in my career but also have taught me lessons about racing that I've continued to apply.

I've talked about racing as a team effort involving trainers, grooms, pony people, gate crew, exercise riders, and hot-walkers, but without a great horse, a jockey is just riding on thin air. Seethreepeo, an enormous white horse, took care of me when I was an apprentice jockey. He was one of Bud Delp's stakes horses because he had an injury to one of his tendons and needed to run lighter (I was still an apprentice, so I carried less weight than the other jockeys). While Seethreepeo was being treated for his tendon injury Bud ran him in a lower class (a class with less formidable horses) so he wouldn't have to run hard. As a result, he blew away most of his competition.

I was lucky to ride Seethreepeo, not because he won but because he was one smart horse. If I was boxed in during a race with nowhere to go, I would push on Seethreepeo's neck to move, sometimes in a less than safe situation. He'd ignore me. Instead, he'd back out of the spot, or as soon as a little hole opened up he'd pull me through. I was a young rider, at times tending to make mistakes because of frustration or too much aggression, but while I was on his back Seethreepeo never allowed me to make dangerous mistakes.

Horses, not just jockeys, can be "diabolical." John Forbes had a horse named Great Fanfare that he ran in Atlantic City and Monmouth. When the gate opened, Great Fanfare would race like a gazelle to the lead. From then on it was stop and go, cat and mouse, all the way to the wire. As long as no other horses were near him, Great Fanfare would race relaxed, his ears straight up in the air. If another horse threatened his lead, however, he would suddenly pin his ears back and charge forward. And that's not all he'd do. Great Fanfare would drift toward that horse, not enough to get me disqualified but enough to take the joy out of the other horse's trip. I learned that I, too, could drift in on other jockeys to keep them from riding too close or to discourage them from trying to pass me.

I almost didn't get to ride Gaily Gaily, one of Bill Mott's most successful stakes horses. In the fall of 1988 I had yet to move to the New York racetracks and was still concentrating most of my efforts in New Jersey. Some days, however, I would ride races at Belmont during the day, and then Snake would drive me to night races at Meadowlands. It was an exhausting schedule, and finally we decided that we would no longer ride the last few races at Belmont or the first at Meadowlands. If we continued to race along the parkway to get to New Jersey in time, we were headed for a major accident. Therefore, when Bill Mott called Snake to ask if I'd ride in a Grade 1 stakes (stakes races involving the most money) called the Flower Bowl Handicap, Snake said he didn't think we'd take the race.

In the Flower Bowl Handicap, each horse is assigned to carry a certain weight according to his talent. Gaily Gaily had been assigned approximately 109 pounds, and I was the only jockey in New York who could ride at that low weight. Bill Mott called back to ask me to ride. "Bill," Snake said, "it's the eighth race at Belmont on a Friday night; the traffic will be a nightmare." Bill asked Snake if he was out of his mind. Riding in a Grade 1 stakes is like playing in the Super Bowl — it's a big deal. Snake was telling Bill that he would rather trade off a stakes horse than get caught in traffic and not make it to Meadowlands in time. We changed our minds, and I rode Gaily Gaily in the Handicap and won. Over the next two and a half years, I continued to ride her, and we won stakes at Keeneland, Belmont, and Arlington, and in Louisiana and Florida.

I learned every quirk that the large, powerful chestnut had, and developed the ability to ride her better than any other jockey. She hated people around her face and head, so when I warmed her up in the post parade I took her away from the pony girl so that she could be alone. Gaily Gaily liked to gallop before entering the starting gate. Her long strides would have fatigued any other horse, and slowing her would have been more stressful for her than letting her run. After galloping to a point on the backside, about an eighth of a mile from the starting gate, Gaily Gaily liked to stand still for five minutes and look at the grandstand. When the other horses from the post parade began to warm up, Gaily Gaily would shake the pressure off with a quick twist of her neck and move toward the post parade. We'd join the other horses, walking right ahead of our pony girl, and Gaily Gaily would enter the starting gate the second time I asked and stand perfectly still.

For all her quirks, Gaily Gaily was a professional. She never sweated the little things. If there was a problem and all the horses had to be backed out of the starting gate, she'd be the only one not upset. Hey, it's just a race, she seemed to be saying to the other horses as she watched their shenanigans. There were times, however, when Gaily Gaily didn't want to run. She'd leave the gate like a sour goat, but once I asked her to move, she'd come on like a train. In the end, she always did what was necessary to win while expending the least amount of energy. I never won a race on Gaily Gaily by more than a neck or a nose, but she taught me to respect her quirks and use them to our advantage.

Rubiano, one of Scotty Schulhofer's horses, was the second Eclipse Award winner I ever rode. (The year-end Eclipse Awards honor the top thoroughbred horses in several categories.) In the early '90s, Sal, Scotty's foreman, would ask me to breeze him when his regular jockey, José Santos, was out of town for a race. "No problem," I'd reply — I was thrilled to ride such a beautiful, well-bred horse. "You know, Sal, someday I'm gonna ride this horse in a race. I can just tell that something great is going to happen between us." "Julie," he'd reply with a smile, "don't be so sentimental and mushy, just breeze the horse." In July, 1992, José Santos had a bad spill, fracturing his right arm and collarbone and cracking his hip. Scotty called Snake and asked if I wanted to ride Rubiano.

If Bart Simpson were a horse, he'd be Rubiano, who is a total brat until he's out of the gate. In the post parade, Rubiano likes to trot about with his neck arched. When it's time to get into the starting gate he has to be pushed in from behind. Once in, he tries to put his leg up on the edge of the gate. But when the announcer yells, "And they're off!" Rubiano breaks fast and runs like a professional. He has an incredible drive to win. So much so that in one stakes race we rode, he leaned over and bit Chris Antley's horse, Diablo, because Diablo was pushing him out of the hole he wanted to surge through. Stop pushing me, buddy, he seemed to snarl as we moved past Chris and Diablo and crossed the wire first. Not only is every horse different, but some are bursting at the seams with spirit and personality.

Consider the Lily was a two-year-old filly with a fuzzy coat from spending time out in the fields. In 1992 I told Allen Jerkens that Consider the Lily was adorable, that I loved her personality and the way she looked. "That thing?" he asked with a laugh. "She's so slow we have to kick her to get her to move, and so quiet I could put a ten-year-old kid on her." But Al smiled at my comments because even though Consider the Lily was just a little baby, I had recognized what he already knew, that Lily was very well bred and would someday evolve into a great racehorse. "Al, please let me gallop her," I begged.

Consider the Lily was a bit naughty, which made me love her. I began to gallop Lily for Al. I would put her behind the other babies so that all the dirt from their hooves would fly back at her. She'd jump about and get angry at me, but she eventually learned to ignore the dirt. When we'd come into the stretch I'd pull her out and let her pass all those horses that kicked dirt in her eyes. When I let her see daylight, her little ears would pin back and she'd charge. Lily became my special project, along with being Al's and just about everyone else's who worked for him. We all put a lot of time into her training.

Consider the Lily was a rebel without a cause. When I first tried to take her into the starting gate, she practically threw herself on the ground. When the gate guys tried to pull her in, she bit and struck at them because they were trying to make her do something she didn't want to do. It took several weeks before that process became smoother. Still, I continued to rave about Consider the Lily to Al. "She's a fat little squirt," he'd say jokingly. "She hasn't even run yet." "When she does run," I replied, "I want to be on her back."

I prepped Consider the Lily before her first race at Saratoga, breezing her behind several horses to get her a little angry and hyped. A few days later, it was time to race. Consider the Lily's first race was five furlongs (five eighths of a mile) on the dirt, and because it was for green (young) horses, nobody wanted to break out of the gate slowly. If their young horses got dirt in their eyes they'd probably jump about and lose the race. We broke from the gate on top and could easily have moved up front, but I chose to place my horse behind two others. Consider the Lily ran fastest when she was placed behind a few horses and then asked to go in the stretch. She was used to the dirt, and she wouldn't sacrifice her race by jumping around.

As we came into the stretch I was smiling. I knew we were

going to win. I let Lily see daylight and began to push on her neck. She tore ahead, the trees and people streaking by us in a blur of color. Consider the Lily won by several lengths. More important, she learned to bide her time, and I had the satisfaction of seeing the results of my savvy.

The second time Consider the Lily ran, I was in the hospital after my disastrous spill in 1993 at Saratoga. From the hospital, where I was being prepped for surgery and given massive doses of morphine and other painkillers, I instructed my valet, Tony, to call the jockey who would replace me as rider and tell him how Consider the Lily liked to be ridden. I just wanted her to keep winning, even if I wasn't on her back. The whole morning before my accident, I'd been excited to have the opportunity to ride Consider the Lily again. I had gone to Al's barn to watch her eat and graze, and talked to him about the race. I just knew that Consider the Lily was going to be a great racehorse.

The day of my accident Consider the Lily didn't finish in the top three, because of an injury to a small bone in her knee. Later Allen joked that Consider the Lily had heard that I was hurt and decided she didn't want to race without me.

– 23 –

TRIPLE CROWN RACES

THE KENTUCKY DERBY: a mile and a quarter at Churchill Downs, Louisville, Kentucky, on the first Saturday in May. The Preakness Stakes: a mile and three-sixteenths at Pimlico Race Course in Baltimore, Maryland, on the second Saturday after the Derby. The Belmont Stakes: a mile and a half at Belmont Park in Elmont, New York, on the third Saturday after the Preakness. They're not just three American races on dirt.

The Triple Crown races are the ultimate jewels in an owner's, trainer's, horse's, and jockey's crown. They are the dream beyond the dream. In 1991 I was given the opportunity by trainer Dave Monaci to ride Subordinated Debt, winner of the Withers Stakes (a large stakes race), at Belmont. I had watched the Belmont for years, first as a kid, then as an apprentice jockey, and eventually as a journeyman. To ride onto the track aboard a great horse to the cheers of thousands of fans was overwhelming.

No jockey in a Triple Crown race plans to lose. No matter what kind of horse they are riding, no matter what the odds, jockeys know in their heart they are going to win. That is the only way to ride — to have unlimited ambition and to show up every day and take a swing, knowing that ultimately there will be a connection. Whether that connection is the result of God's grace, fate, luck, or persistence will never be known. On the first Saturday in June, I rode Subordinated Debt over to the starting gate with a thundering heart and a mouth dry with anticipation. I was going to win.

Subordinated Debt's nickname is Sad Sack. He's a very capable horse, but is so quiet in training that neither a jockey nor a trainer can be sure of how he will race on any given day. Although Subordinated Debt was not my favorite horse, I liked him, just as I like all the horses I ride, and felt confident that if he ran his best, we had a shot at a Triple Crown race. The only strategy I applied during the race was to stay in the middle and make sure I had some horse to finish with. It's hard to have much of a strategy in a mile-and-a-half race, because it's so long and there are too many horses to be able to handicap effectively.

He ran well. That is, for the first mile or so. Then Subordinated Debt began to fade. There was no big secret or complications to the race, he just didn't run well that day. I had ridden him to the best of my ability, but it was not enough. We finished in ninth place. I was disappointed, but I still remember that first Belmont as a magical time when one of my dreams materialized. One year later, I was again fortunate to ride in the Belmont, aboard a horse named Colony Light. In that race we finished sixth.

My first Kentucky Derby was in 1992. Riding onto the track in the post parade at Churchill Downs to the strains of "My Old Kentucky Home" was spellbinding. I just wanted to stop my horse and stare at the thousands in the grandstand and the other horses and riders surrounding me. I had seen my first live Derby the spring I worked as a groom for Clarence Picou. I'd crouched on the top of his barn, watching the race and imagining that someday I would be aboard a magnificent athlete tearing down the stretch to win the Kentucky Derby by a nose.

I wasn't even scheduled to ride in the '92 Derby. While I'd been offered a few opportunities, Snake had turned them all down. He didn't want me to ride any slow horses. There are too many good stakes horses to ride the weekend of the Derby to ride a 20 to 1 long shot. If it had been up to me, I would have ridden any of those horses we'd been offered in order to be in the Kentucky Derby, but Snake likes me to ride only horses that finish at the top. That's his job, and just as he watches me ride without comment, I let him take care of our best interests without argument.

Two weeks before the Derby I was offered an opportunity to ride a horse that had a shot at it. The jockey who had originally been chosen to ride couldn't because of an alleged drug problem. Snake agreed to let me race. Once again, no big story. My horse warmed up fairly well, but diminished quickly in the race.

Strike two for the Triple Crown? That's not how I felt. In both the '91 and '92 Belmont and the '92 Kentucky Derby I felt lucky to have been given the opportunity to ride capable horses and to experience the electricity of Triple Crown races. Losing a race is always disappointing, but no jockey can plan her road to success or pathway to failure. All a jockey can do is show up every day and try to do her best.

I began to ride trainer Scotty Schulhofer's Colonial Affair in 1991 when he was a two-year-old baby. He was so full of life. He'd rear on his hind legs, not to throw me off, but to show his youth and happiness. He was an honest horse, meaning he'd show his free spirit but always played straight and never tried to dump his rider. Colonial Affair reminded me of my pony Filly, and I loved him for his spunk and for his ability, even at a young age, to get down to business when required. When I breezed Colonial Affair, he was no longer a goofy character but a pumped-up, powerful creature.

I knew he was special. The day of Colonial Affair's second race I was scheduled to ride a race out of town. I asked Scotty to put my friend Richie Migliore on Colonial Affair for the race. Scotty checked with the owner, Don Little, and both agreed that Richie could ride the horse. "Richie," I said before I left town, "today you're going to break the maiden of the '93 Belmont Stakes winner" (Colonial Affair hadn't won a race yet). Richie laughed, then said, "Okay, can I ride him in the Belmont, too?" "Just break his maiden," I replied. I had plans of my own to ride Colonial Affair in the Belmont.

Richie won, and Colonial Affair continued to perform well, but Scotty decided to give him a little time off from the races and to train him with blinkers because he was still clowning around too much on the track. After four months off, Colonial Affair returned mature and powerful, performing like a rocket on the track. Scotty planned to enter Colonial Affair in the Peter Pan, a prep race before the '93 Belmont, and I was looking forward to the race with confidence.

"I really screwed up, Scotty," I said, dismounting Colonial Affair after finishing in the Peter Pan a disappointing second. "It was all my fault. I pushed him early to get a good position, and I should have kept him from moving forward too quickly. Once he moved, I was obligated to maintain the continuity of our race." In the stretch we were beaten by a marvelous Allen Jerkens horse, Virginia Rapids. "Scotty, I'm sorry." Scotty told me that when a jockey is learning a horse, it's impossible to always judge his strength correctly. He told me that I'd have another chance to prove that Colonial Affair and I were a great team.

I was lucky that Scotty and Colonial Affair's owner, Centennial Farms and Don Little, were so understanding, and lucky that they still wanted me to ride him in the Belmont.

The day of the 1993 Belmont Stakes, Colonial Affair walked around the barn like he was better than sliced bread. He was one of the least-raced horses to run in the '93 Belmont — before that he'd been in only a handful of races — but he had the maturity and poise of a much more traveled horse. On that first Saturday in June, he was feeling his oats. And I was feeling mine.

"Hey, George, what's it gonna feel like this afternoon when I have that blanket of carnations laid over my lap in the winner's circle?" I asked one of Scotty's exercise riders. George Martens had won the Belmont before retiring and coming to work for Scotty. He just smiled and said, "Well, Julie, it feels good." Scotty called over, "You'll find out this afternoon, Krone." In my heart, I thought he was right.

After handicapping all my races for the day of the Belmont, I tried to make my schedule as normal as possible. I took a nap.

It's important not to make big race days too rushed or crazy. Tony came into the jocks' room with my tack, and I asked him to get me five programs with all the jockeys' signatures on the covers. He asked me why. "Because I'm going to want them as souvenirs when I win this race," I replied. Tony is a bit superstitious, and he warned me not to say that. "It's okay, Tony," I said, "I really am going to win."

"Please don't make me do this interview," I begged a reporter who had scheduled an interview with me right before I was supposed to go into the paddock and mount up for the Belmont Stakes. I was worried that I wouldn't make it into the paddock within the allotted time limit. The reporter let me go. I raced past Scotty and Mr. Little to Colonial Affair and ended up being in the paddock so early that I had to wait twenty-five minutes before mounting my horse.

I walked around the paddock looking at the other horses. They were all the result of years of superb breeding and training. I stood looking at Prairie Bayou, jockey Mike Smith's mount and winner of the Preakness. He was just magnificent. I noticed which horses seemed more nervous, felt their excitement, and calculated their possibilities of diminishing in the stretch because their nervous energy was being wasted in the paddock. Finally it was time to mount my horse. After I got a leg up, I patted Colonial Affair on the neck and said, "Let's go make history, buddy."

Colonial Affair loves a crowd. He arched his neck and tiptoed through the paddock to the track, stomping the ground once in a while to show he was pumped and ready. I began to feel a bit more relaxed as we moved out into the post parade.

A normal post parade lasts ten to twelve minutes, but because of delays the Belmont post parade ended up being only four minutes. When we reached the track, Colonial Affair, our pony girl, and I got right down to business.

The post parade was important for Colonial Affair. He is a very playful horse, but if he is disciplined during the parade, he can immediately become very shy, sometimes for days. I knew that I had to let him be a playboy, because he would feel better about himself and run faster if he felt happy and strong. I wanted Colonial Affair after the post parade to feel like he could knock down the Empire State Building. During those four minutes, the pony girl (who also understood Colonial Affair's personality) and I were careful not to let him bite at our legs, so we wouldn't have to reprimand him. By the time we entered the starting gate, Colonial Affair was feeling unbeatable.

He stood beautifully in the gate. We were one of the low numbers, so I had time to scan the other horses as they entered the gate, and refresh my memory of who had speed. I knew I didn't want to get too far back early on, because if I got behind a bad bunch of horses that weren't competitive, I wouldn't be able to move up.

We broke fast, and Colonial Affair got his feet under him very quickly. He was immediately in my hands, not pulling too hard, just perfectly balanced. We moved around the track like clockwork. Colonial Affair was right on that day. He indicated to me that all I needed to do was just let him know when I wanted to go faster. I waited, conserving his energy for the backstretch. I was determined not to make the same mistake I'd made in the Peter Pan.

On the backstretch Colonial Affair got a bit discouraged. I had been on the inside the whole race, where the dirt kicks back hard from the horses in front. Both riders and horses get used to the dirt, but it still hurts. Colonial Affair began to drop the bridle a bit. When I pushed him he still had energy, but he was no longer pulling. I had to get him to the outside. My opportunity came milliseconds later when I spied a small gap. I quickly moved him into the gap, which was a little tight but turned out to be the right move. He did end up with a small cut on the back of his leg from another horse's hoof, but his well-being was never endangered. We moved to the outside, and Colonial Affair blinked his eyes clear of the dirt, grabbed the bridle, and told me, Let's get on with it.

We were three quarters of the way through the Belmont, and Colonial Affair wanted to get busy. There were nine horses in front of us when we made our move on the backstretch. I saw all the jockeys pushing hard on the necks of their horses. I hadn't even begun to ask for Colonial Affair's reserves. We moved up to jockey Jerry Bailey. Jerry has great timing and has won a lot of big stakes races. My position couldn't have been better, I thought. Even if I second-guessed my own timing, I felt pretty confident of Jerry's. We moved ahead of Jerry, and as I watched the rest of the jockeys pushing their horses to the limit I realized that Colonial Affair and I were going to win. I began to push on Colonial Affair as we moved into the stretch. I chirped to him and threw my reins, and he sprouted wings. He flew down the stretch, continuing to accelerate as he raced toward the wire.

When we crossed the wire, my mind went blank. All I could hear was a tiny voice inside me saying, "We won the Belmont, we won the Belmont, . . ." Colonial Affair kept galloping after the wire. A lot of times jockeys who win big races will stand up and wave to the crowd as their horse continues to gallop up the track. I recognized immediately how tired my horse was, though, so instead of rising and waving I turned my attention to Colonial Affair, who was pulling on the reins a bit and asking me to help him balance. We slowed, and I began to pat his neck until his ears came up and he relaxed. Then I glanced back down the track, a habit all jockeys have of scanning the track to make sure none of their friends are hurt. I saw an ambulance on the backside and my heart sank.

"Who is it, Tom?" I asked my outrider. "Mike Smith," he replied. I closed my eyes and said a quick prayer — Please, God, let Mike be okay. . . . I know you take care of animals, too, so please, God, let Prairie Bayou be okay, too. Then I went to the scales to make my win official, remounted Colonial Affair, and rode to the winner's circle as the first female winner of a Triple Crown race in the history of the sport. I shook hands with Don Little, Scotty, and Tony. It seemed as if I was sur-rounded by a wall of congratulations. And when they laid the blanket of white carnations over my lap, the perfume of the flowers overwhelmed me along with the realization that I had won a Triple Crown race.

The only thing after the Belmont that could wipe the smile off my face was seeing Mike Smith's devastation when the horse he loved, Prairie Bayou, had to be destroyed after taking a misstep and falling during the race, resulting in a broken front cannon bone. It was a tragedy for Prairie Bayou, his owner, and his trainer, and for Mike, who had ridden him since he was a baby and truly loved him.

Mike Smith showed inordinate grace and composure in both dealing with his own loss and answering all the questions the media desperately wanted to put to him. "I just need a half hour or so to take a shower and then I'll be back outside to talk to all of you," he said softly to the media. Mike was wrenched inside, but he knew that it was the media's responsibility to find out what had happened to Prairie Bayou and that it was his job to tell them. A half hour later he emerged from the jockeys' room, still distraught but ready to talk. And he did talk, with a natural honesty and bravery that I will never forget. Mike told the reporters that Prairie Bayou's breakdown "came out of nowhere. It was a bad step; it was raining and kind of slippery. Everything was normal; it was just an abnormal mishap." Then he cried, and through his tears he explained that what had happened was a horrible tragedy and that he was really hurting. This is my livelihood, he said, and I will go on, but right now I need some time to get over this.

It would take me a long time to learn how to deal with the media as honestly as Mike had. I spent years trying to prove how tough a rider I was, trying to show the world that male or female, I was a talent. To show any weakness felt like failure to me. Eventually I would learn that Mike's openness was the only way to work with the media, and that shrugging off the burden of always being happy, positive, and never showing vulnerability would feel like taking fifty pounds off my back.

– 24 –

LIGHTS AND CAMERAS

$53,890,976. THAT SUM was my total career earnings (I receive a percentage of those earnings) by the spring of 1993. I would never say that the money wasn't a nice reward for my efforts, which include not only an incredible amount of hard work but also willingly mangling my body and risking my life every day on the track. It isn't the money that I most value, though.

I was the first and only female jockey to ride in the Belmont Stakes in 1991, and to win the Belmont, in 1993. I was the first woman to compete in a Breeders' Cup race; to win more than 2,800 races in a career, becoming the winningest female jockey in the sport; the first woman to surpass the $50 million plateau in career purse earnings; to win riding titles at major racetracks, including four consecutive years as leading rider at Meadowlands (1987–1990), and three straight years (1987–1989) at Monmouth Park. I have been in the top twelve jockeys nationally in earnings for four years, and in 1992 was ninth in earnings. I rode six winners in one day at both Monmouth Park and Meadowlands, and five winners in a day at Saratoga.

In 1989 I appeared on the cover of *Sports Illustrated.* And in 1993 I was named ABC News "Person of the Week" and featured on ABC's *World News Tonight* with Peter Jennings. The Sudafed Sportswoman of the Year Award was also presented to me in 1993. A month later I joined *Glamour* magazine's Ten Women of the Year along with Supreme Court Justice Ruth Bader Ginsburg, U.S. Attorney General Janet Reno, U.S. Surgeon General Joycelyn Elders, New York Assistant District Attorney Linda Fairstein and American Red Cross President Elizabeth Hanford Dole. The following year I was selected as one of five Women of the Year by CBS News. I've visited both President George Bush and his wife, Barbara, Tipper Gore, and President Bill Clinton as a member of the Women's Sports Foundation and recipient of its outstanding-female-athlete-of-the-year award. And, on March 8, 1994, I was awarded the ESPY Award as the Outstanding Female Athlete of 1993. In addition, I've appeared several times on *Late Night with David Letterman, The Tonight Show* with Johnny Carson, and *Live with Regis & Kathie Lee.*

The money, accomplishments, honors, and awards have meant much more than their face value. Just as trainers, fellow jockeys, and racetrack officials provided my early education not only as an athlete but also as an empathetic, trustworthy, talented person, those later honors gave me a truer understanding of my responsibilities as a personality in sports and a role model to children. They also allowed me to grow into someone I like.

Although I'd had athletic accomplishments, I was still a little kid from Eau Claire, Michigan, and I had a lot to learn about preparation for appearances, public speaking, and poise. I lacked confidence in all those areas, something I was determined to rectify. It is better to be prepared when giving a speech than to speak off the cuff. That was my first lesson when I began to do television and radio interviews. I discovered that when I was organized and prepared I wouldn't walk away from the experience thinking, Gosh, I wish I'd said this or hadn't mentioned that.

Sue Finley and Dan Leary, publicity and public relations professionals at the New York Racing Association, have helped me both with my public appearances and in organizing my thoughts before speeches. They were the ones who arranged for my first appearance on David Letterman's show, an experience I was to repeat two more times and will always cherish. I love Dave's show and was genuinely flipped out that I was actually going to be a guest.

My first appearance was in 1989, right after I broke my arm. I arrived at the show early and waited in the "green room" to go into makeup. Someone came in to talk to me about what I was going to say, and to warn me that even though I was supposed to talk about my accident I shouldn't be too gruesome, because David gets queasy. Then I was taken to makeup, and was thrilled to see Chevy Chase rising from the chair. I said something dumb to him like, "Boy, you've sure made me laugh a lot." Chevy thanked me, and we spoke for several minutes. "I'm going to let you in on a running joke I have with Dave," Chevy confided. He told me that he was going to say to Dave, "Is that a burrito in your pocket or are you just happy to see me?" He told me that when I walked on stage, I should say the same thing. Then he gave me one of those really cool Chevy

Chase smiles and walked off. I can't say something like that with millions of people watching, I thought.

I was very nervous as I walked onto the soundstage and took my seat beside David. I leaned over and said what Chevy had told me. David broke up laughing, "No, it's not a burrito, Julie," he replied. The interview went wonderfully. He is an incredible interviewer, with a real talent for helping his guests create a flow of stories. If he didn't have that ability, I would have appeared a lesser athlete and person. It was the first time I realized what a difference a great interviewer makes. And it wasn't only Dave but his entire staff working together, much as the grooms, hot-walkers, jockeys, and trainers do at the track, that made the experience so positive and enjoyable. Of course, during that first show I played up my injury, telling David how the bones crunched and ground — which I've done on his show in all my later appearances (which usually coincide with accidents and the resulting time off) and which always makes Dave grimace and laugh.

Johnny Carson was a great interviewer, too. What I re-member most about appearing on his show was seeing him for the first time in the wings. His back was turned to me and he was wearing a dress shirt without the jacket. Boy, I thought, that's a really cute guy, nicely built, with a small waist and long legs. Then Johnny turned around and I was shocked to see his face and not a young man's.

Sue Finley and Dan Leary helped me to develop the con-fidence to appear on national television and the ability to speak well with interviewers, but no one could help me with one of my most embarrassing moments, at the White House. In con-junction with the Women's Sports Foundation, I was receiving an outstanding-female-athlete award along with a group of other talented women. Both George and Barbara Bush were present, and as each award was given out we were called up to receive it. When my turn came, I walked forward and handed President Bush a shoe from Kentucky Derby winner Winning Colors. I told President Bush that Winning Colors had a message for him, then I whinnied, and the photographer snapped a photo of us laughing together. Everything was going well until we all moved to the Oval Office for autographs.

I kicked Millie. I didn't just kick her; I stumbled over her and almost fell on my face — and she was pregnant at the time. I don't know if the president or his wife saw it, but several other people did and shook their heads disapprovingly. It didn't ruin the experience, nothing could do that, but I did think to myself, I've worked so hard to speak well, to speak grammatically, slowly, and eloquently, and then I go and trip over America's most-loved dog.

In 1994 I returned to the White House with the Women's Sports Foundation, and I was constantly on the lookout for Socks. I wasn't going to make the same mistake. But I recognize now that mistakes are a part of what I do. That being a sports personality doesn't disqualify me from being a person, someone with good days and bad days, someone who is heartbroken by the loss of a boyfriend or a big race, or the news of a loved one's illness. The only difference between being a sports personality as opposed to simply a person is that I have a responsibility to share many of my heartbreaks with the media. For that I have to show my vulnerability, which for me was a hard-learned lesson.

– 25 –

PRESS STRESS

WHENEVER AN ATHLETE gains fame and fortune there is always someone who takes it upon themselves to be the bane of her existence. For me, that person was John Swenson.

John Swenson was the columnist who wrote "Through the Binoculars," a racing column, for the *New York Post*. On Wednesday, August 25, 1993, he wrote about the NYRA's decision to use me to promote New York racing. He labeled their use of me the "Kronization" of the sport. Following are excerpts from that column.

> *Despairing of a way to make [racing] more attractive to the public, NYRA is trying to sell Krone . . . as the dominant personality . . . who will bring new fans to the sport. . . .*
>
> *Krone is not the best rider out there . . . [but] is routinely referred to as a "superstar." . . .*
>
> *Krone has interpreted this lack of criticism from the local*

press as proof of her divine right to declare herself bigger than the game. . . .

The Kronization of racing in New York is creating a schism. Krone has her legion of devoted followers, but she is also resented in many places around the track due to the perception that there is a double standard applied to her because she is "good for racing." . . .

Krone is not "good for racing." She is good for Julie Krone. . . .

John Swenson obviously did not like me. I believe his dislike stemmed more from his lack of understanding of racing than from his personal distaste for Julie Krone, since we had never been introduced during his time on staff at the *Post*. Unfortunately, Mr. Swenson had an outlet for his confusion and hostility, and his column reflected predominantly the negative side of racing. The following is an example of a race and my version of how John Swenson would interpret and write about that race.

Let's say I have a nervous, frail, turf filly, and when I pull on her reins to slow her down and the bit touches her mouth, her reaction is to throw her head in the air. In the starting gate, I have to break slowly and put my hands down on her neck so the reins are long and she is enticed to relax. Before the race her trainer, too, worked with her and had her galloped on an extremely long rein to help her relax, and the grooms and hotwalkers worked quietly and calmly with her.

My filly has a lot of speed, but normally she breaks from the gate fast and then diminishes at the end because she has used too much nervous energy. The entire stable is working with her to solve this problem and make her a quality horse. Julie, don't let her go to the front, the owner and trainer warn before I move to the gate. We want you to teach that filly to bide her time. When I break from the gate I don't push my body or hands really hard. I break softly and then settle my hands on her neck. The filly wants to run faster, and I'm forced to pull on her reins, which makes her throw her head. I drop behind several horses to save ground, and get too close to a horse's heels in front of me, so I have to check her again. Now the filly throws her head even higher, giving the impression that I'm steadying her, which is not the case. I continue to pull the filly back from the lead horse, beginning a battle that will eventually exhaust her. She is learning that she can't bust out of the starting gate and run right to the lead. We are teaching her to run at the end of the race instead of wasting all her energy right out of the gate. Learning that lesson is extremely important to her future success.

The race isn't over. We hit the backside and the pace picks up a bit. I drop my hands and she goes with the pace. I stay on the inside, waiting for an opportunity to get out with a small filly that can't really push the other horses around. I get boxed in, and at the last minute pull through a small hole and get beaten by a head at the wire. I'm happy, the trainer and owner are happy, and the filly has run well and learned a lesson. I know that I've ridden my best, even risking my life to squeeze through a hole in the last second of the race.

After the race, I can imagine John Swenson going upstairs and looking at the racing form. He sees that there is no speed in the race, except for my filly. He might think, Well, Krone should have been in the lead right from the gate. Julie Krone should have won, because her horse had the speed, so she must have ridden her poorly. Then he might write something like the following in the paper: "Julie Krone broke on favorite. She was the only speed in the race, but instead of surging ahead she chose to wrestle and fight with her horse and fell behind. Krone checked her horse in the first turn and then continued to keep her filly in trouble for the entire race. Still, she almost won, solely based on the horse's talent, not her own."

John Swenson doesn't appear to understand the theory behind building a racehorse. Had I busted out of the starting gate and ridden that little filly until her eyes were bugging out of her head and she was so freaked out from the race that she hated it, Swenson would have seen a good race. He would have seen a good race even though my horse would have finished farther back, diminished as she always had, and been beaten in double figures at the end of the race. Swenson probably wouldn't have understood that I finished with less of a horse than I began with. It's not that I didn't want to win. I did, but in the confines of what is best for the horse. The bottom line is that I (as well as all successful jockeys) have mangled my body to win races. Trainers and owners spend twenty hours a day working with their horses so that they can win. Why would either of us want to do anything but win?

And it's not only me, although I was a particular target for Swenson. When he was not pointing out my personal and professional faults, he spent his spare time bashing jockeys like

Chris Antley, writing that Chris continues to be unable to break out of the starting gate well and that Richie Migliore, after breaking his neck the previous summer, was afraid to go through a hole at the eighth-pole and that if he hadn't been he would have won. He also attacked bug riders, shattering their newfound fragile confidence.

John Swenson used his column to wage personal battles against jockeys, owners, and trainers. And the things he wrote were powerful and at times painful. Worst of all, Swenson's column sometimes negated all the hard work that we (jockeys, trainers, grooms, hot-walkers, owners) put into every horse.

In April, 1994, I finally met John Swenson. He was sitting backstage at a concert, and a friend pointed him out to me. I walked right over to him and shook his hand. I was genuinely pleased to have the chance to meet him and clear up some of the misunderstandings we'd had in the past. Before the evening was over, we were posing for pictures together. I guess the entire experience was a good lesson for both of us on confronting difficulties instead of making assumptions. It would not be my last lesson on working with individuals in the media.

On August 21, 1993, I rode Colonial Affair in the Travers Stakes at Saratoga. I was the first female jockey to ride in that race, and I was aboard a horse who had just won the Belmont and was favored to win. We didn't. When I returned to the jockeys' room, there was a group of reporters waiting for me. I was so incredibly disappointed in my own performance that I brushed past them and headed inside. For the next forty minutes I sat with my arms wrapped tightly around my legs, just staring off into space. A few jockeys stopped by me and all I could say was, "Did I ride him that bad? Did I cost him the race?" "Julie, stop being like that," they all said. But I couldn't help it. I loved Colonial Affair and believed in his abilities, and we should have won the Travers. I sat in the jocks' room until the last race. When I finally walked out to the reporters, all I said was, "Colonial Affair ran really well and I'm proud of him." Then I strode away.

I hadn't wanted to show my disappointment to those reporters. I didn't want them to see that I was upset, but I was wrong. The media's job is to report a jockey's version of a race, win or lose, and they were just trying to do that job. And it's my job to tell them and all the racing fans my version of what happens. Mike Smith did that eloquently and courageously when Prairie Bayou broke down in the Belmont. Unfortunately, I hadn't learned that lesson.

"I waited forty minutes to speak to Julie Krone, and when she came out of the jockeys' room all she said was that she was proud of Colonial Affair," I heard a reporter say as he left the track that evening. I confronted him, which was all wrong, but at the time I felt like he should have a little sympathy for me. Bill Finley, a member of the media, pulled me aside. "Listen to me," he said. "You can't handle yourself that way." "Bill, I'm just really upset, and when that reporter wanted to talk to me I was still feeling dysfunctional and hurt by the whole thing. I didn't know what to say. . . ." "Julie," Bill replied, "how 'bout just saying the truth."

The concept of admitting my weaknesses, letting people know that I was sad that Colonial Affair hadn't won the race, was still extremely difficult for me. I thought about what Bill said for several days, and I knew in my heart that he was right. It was too exhausting trying to be perfect for the media anyway. But it wasn't until my spill at Saratoga in 1993 that I acted on Bill's advice.

– 26 –

THE DEVIL DIDN'T DO IT

IF I COULD have taken Bill Finley's advice and told the media the truth at Saratoga on August 30, 1993, I would have said that the pain was so bad that I wanted to die. But on that day no one asked if they could put me out of my misery, and I was too busy screaming to tell the media anything. I had shattered my right ankle, suffered a cardiac contusion (bruised heart), and punctured the inside of my left elbow, exposing the joint. And as I lay in the ambulance on the way to the hospital, I prayed to God that I would pass out.

Every few minutes Tony asked me if I wanted him to hold my ankle. I was holding it myself, after refusing to let the paramedic take off my boot and wrap an air cast around my leg. I'd say, "Yeah, yeah, yeah," then when he got near it I'd scream "No!" I held my own ankle for the whole ride. At times I yelled at the paramedic to stop touching it, but he wasn't even near it. I was just hallucinating with pain. Also in the ambulance were friends who tried to keep my mind off the pain by telling me stories. Nothing could make me forget the pain. The ride to the hospital was only seven minutes, but I swear it lasted hours.

The first thing the doctor did was give me morphine. He didn't even try to get my boot off until the painkiller had begun to work. "Let Tony do it! Let Tony do it!" I screamed as the doctor approached me with scissors. Tony removed my boots every day; he knew where the weak parts were on the seams. I stared with venom at the doctor and said, "Tony always takes my boots off." After looking at my face, the doctor handed his scissors to Tony, who assumed that there was no way that doctor was going to let him near me. "Oh God," he said when he wasn't stopped, "I'm really gonna do this." He did a great job. Tony understood where my ankle hurt and how to manipulate my boot. And when he finally did cut it off, he did it in an entirely different way than the paramedic had first attempted.

The painkiller kicked in, and for a few minutes everything was a blur. White coats, doctors' and nurses' voices, the faces of people I knew were my friends. Twenty minutes later, the morphine shot wore off. I have a very fast metabolism for pain medication. The doctors had to alter their regular morphine schedule to medicate me. Even with the morphine, the agony was unbearable. I remember I was sweating a lot, and crying. There were so many friends around me, supporting me, but nothing mattered but the pain. Then I saw Angel.

Angel Cordero, my friend and one of the greatest jockeys in the world, was there. When I saw his face through the crowd I knew I had to be really hurt. He looked stricken. Angel's eyes moved from my face to my body, then quickly darted back to my face. He'd seen something he didn't want to see. I grabbed his hand for a moment. I needed to touch him, to touch some of the strength he'd had through his accidents and hospital-izations. Later he told me that I'd held his hand so hard that he thought I'd broken one of his fingers. I don't remember doing that, but I do know that having Angel there did something for me. For me, he really represents overcoming pain, being con-sistent, incredibly competitive, and "diabolical." I needed the strength of those memories.

When Angel left, I lay in the hospital bed thinking about how lucky I was to have him as a friend. He has always been an inspiration and source of strength for me while bringing out my competitiveness. When he'd heard that I'd fallen, he'd rushed from the paddock at Saratoga to see me. That made me feel really good.

Then there was John Forbes, a friend whom I both love and respect. He sat by my bedside explaining that following the first operation, he, Snake, and several other friends had ar-ranged to have me flown to Staten Island for additional surgery by Dr. Frank Ariosta, the director of orthopedic surgery of Staten Island University Hospital. It meant so much to me to have John there.

I don't remember my first surgery at Saratoga Hospital. I was told that a Dr. Gallagher had stabilized my ankle joint to alleviate some of the pain that the fractured tibia and fibula bones in my right leg were creating. When I awoke the pain was still there, but it no longer took my breath away. I do, however, remember the flight to Staten Island as a nightmare. In order to fit me through the doorway of the double prop jet, the attendants had to put me in a soft stretcher and then squeeze the stretcher together, cocoonlike. Once they got me into the jet, Tony and the pilot had to climb over me to get to their seats. I was twisted sideways because the plane was so small, and nothing on the stretcher stabilized me so that I didn't have to put pressure on my arm or leg to hold myself steady. I couldn't breathe, and I was crying. When the jet landed, I was transported to an ambulance. Then bumpity, bumpity, bump all the way to the hospital.

That night I was awakened every fifteen minutes. The whole night, every fifteen minutes. Miscellaneous people kept coming into the room to ask questions and introduce themselves. "Hi, I saw you at Belmont," they'd say. I was beside myself with pain and exhaustion. After a while, people would come in and before they could say anything I'd snap, "What do you want? Please leave me alone." The situation would have bothered any person, regardless of whether or not they were critically injured.

I had a bad hospital stay. My epidural, an IV that transports painkillers, fell out twice, leaving me for hours in agonizing pain. The second time it was replaced there was a small release of painkiller that went into my spinal cord and traveled to my brain. That was quite a trip. My eyeballs rolled around independently for a while. My right eye would roll up and my left eye would roll down. I looked like a Saturday-morning cartoon character. One morning there was a mix-up with my epidural and one of the interns thought I'd been given too much morphine. He shot Narcan into my IV to counteract the morphine — Narcan is a drug used on patients who come in off the streets and are so high they have to be brought down quickly.

The intern shot the Narcan in fast and — *boosh* — it hit my brain. My face became immediately flushed, and a powerful surge of gravity sucked me down into my bed. My feet seemed to flip over my head, and I faded in and out of consciousness, awakened by my own convulsions. I thought I was dying. My blood pressure dropped drastically, and I remember hearing the intern say, "Okay, you should be feeling better in a few more moments." I could detect worry both in his voice and on the faces of the nurses.

No one was there to protect me. My mother and Paula Freundlich, both of whom rarely left my side during the ordeal, had gone to the cafeteria for coffee. Whatever drug was later used to counteract the Narcan made me extremely weak and sick for two days. There is a saying that hospitals are very dangerous places. It's true. Basically, everyone who works at a hospital is trying to do their best for the patients, but I can vouch that I saw the same interns for two days straight before they ever went home to sleep. You can't do your best for anyone when you're dead on your feet. And the nurses — well, I found that maybe four out of seven actually took the time, or had the time, to listen to what was hurting me, to understand it, and to get me relief.

"I want to go home . . . my room is yellow . . . my cat misses me . . . stop poking . . . stop poking," I sobbed as an intern tried to find a vein in my arm that wasn't either collapsed or so badly bruised that it was impossible to get the IV in. In an act of frustration, my mother raced into the hallway, grabbed some dishes off a cart, and smashed them onto the floor. I was hurting, and she was helpless.

The night before my second surgery, Tony visited me. In his arms he carried an enormous framed placard of my five winners at Saratoga. He hung it on my wall so that I could look at it that night. My walls were already covered with cards and letters from fans (I received eighty pounds of mail during my one-month stay), as well as beautiful photos that race photographer Barbara Livingston sent to me every day along with a funny note. All the support I received truly helped me to get well. My battle, however, was not just with the pain but with the Devil himself.

For four nights before my surgery I saw the Devil. Granted, I was on so many painkillers that I wouldn't have been surprised to see Santa Claus sitting on the end of my bed, but that didn't make the experience any less terrifying. I went to sleep on those nights, and the Devil appeared. He walked down a long corridor, and I knew he was trying to get somewhere he shouldn't go. I raced behind him, pulling at his clothing to stop him. The clothes were so old and worn that they tore into shreds in my hands. Then he turned and snarled at me, his face taking different forms. Sometimes his tongue was black, sometimes he had dark hair, a tail, and an extra arm. Every night I begged, "Don't go there, don't look in the drawers." And every night he'd reach the room I didn't want him to enter.

It was Mr. Down's high school art class. I raced in front of the Devil and held a cross before him as he entered the room. He pushed it aside and strode to the large orange art drawers that held my entire life. Each drawer contained something important to me — my mother, religion, racing, special times with my father, dear friends. They were all represented by colors. Lori Probst Skinner and I were yellow. Mom and I were blue. The Devil pulled open each drawer and withdrew the colors. Once he touched them, they were no longer the same.

After each visitation, I woke up screaming and told my mother that the Devil was in my room. My mom would get out of her cot and turn on the light, and the Devil would leap into her bed, smiling horrifically at me. My mother couldn't see him, but I knew he was there.

By the second night of the visitations I was hysterical. I couldn't close my eyes without seeing him, and I couldn't stop him from getting to that room and going through my drawers. I asked my mother to bring my Bible to the hospital. Every night I read the Bible with the hospital chaplain. And before I closed my eyes I'd pray to God that the Devil wouldn't visit me that night. I had my mom put signs on my wall that read, "Jesus loves me," and one of the nurses sang "Jesus Loves Me" and "Rejoice" in a beautiful voice to calm my fears. Still, the Devil visited, not just at night, but sometimes in the bright light of day.

No one told me I was hallucinating. My mother, my friends, the nurses all listened to me and accepted my visions. Turn to God, they advised. One dear friend in particular, the late owner Thomas Valando, was incredibly consoling during that time. It was difficult to share my dreams with him; I was afraid that he might think I was delirious. But he didn't. Instead, he talked to me about having faith in God. And my grandparents had instilled such a love of God in me that I was able to turn to Him for help, and by the fourth night, the night before my final ankle surgery, the Devil left my dreams, never to return.

Before my accident, hospital stay, and experience with the Devil, I had been at the point in my life where I was almost ready to take Bill Finley's advice and give up the perfect little jockey image. Over the following month, my entire life would change. I would learn to speak the truth, to turn to support from family and friends, and to accept myself, the good and bad, without reservation. I would spend time with Dr. Robert Pannullo, a wonderful friend who helped care for me in the hospital, and his family. And although my spill at Saratoga, my ankle surgeries, and my recuperation are probably the most painful experiences of my life, I'd go through them again in order to come out on the other side.

– 27 –

RECOVERY

I REMEMBER MY second ankle surgery well. On September 9, 1993, Paula Freundlich held my hand as I was wheeled into the waiting room. I had to pee every three minutes because I was so nervous. A half hour after we arrived, I was wheeled into the operating room, and was reassured to see a familiar face, race-horse owner and anesthesiologist Dr. John Rottkamp, waiting for me with another physician. They walked me through the entire anesthesia process with compassion. As I lay on the operating table waiting for Dr. Ariosta and his team of ortho-pedic surgeons, I felt a sense of calm wash over me. I knew everything was going to be fine, because those doctors are so talented that they would deal completely with every aspect of my injuries. Still, when Dr. Rottkamp said he was going to put me to sleep, I cried.

Two metal plates and fourteen screws were inserted to hold my broken ankle bones together. I remember feeling better when I awoke from surgery, and I think it's because of the way those doctors put me to sleep. I was frightened, but I still felt safe and cared for with them. I awoke and thought, Where's Snigglefritz? Who took care of my trunks and tack? Then I relaxed and remembered all my friends. My mom, Tony and Snake, John and Angel, Pete and Paula Freundlich, and all the people who really care about me and love me. It was the first time I realized how much they had done for me, how they all did their very best to take care of me. It felt wonderfully warm to lie there for a moment and bask in that love, to think about Angel again — to realize that he's Angel Cordero and I'm Julie Krone, and I'm okay.

During the month I spent in the hospital, I had plenty of time to think about the race, and Jorge Chavez, the jockey who was riding Two Is Trouble, the filly that struck me in the chest. My friends told me that after the race Jorge was terribly upset. He just kept saying, "I hit her. She landed right in front of me. I hit her. I ran over her. I hit her. She could be dead. I ran right over her. Is she dead?" There was no way that Jorge could have avoided me. It would have been impossible. I knew that, and even though he probably rationally knew it, he needed to hear it from me. I wrote him a really obnoxious, funny letter telling him not to feel guilty for running me over. Since his horse had struck me, he hadn't won many races. The day he got that letter he won four, including three in a row.

After all the surgeries, when I could finally concentrate without the pain and the mind-dulling pain killers, Dr. Ariosta and I had a conversation about my condition and his prognosis. The first thing he told me was that if I hadn't been wearing my protective vest I might not have survived — the cardiac contusion could have been a fatal blow. He promised me that I would ride again, possibly in six months. I believed him, not only because Dr. Ariosta is incredibly talented but also because his whole persona inspires confidence. There is a brazen roughness to Dr. Ariosta, and beneath it all a tender heart. But although I had faith in Dr. Ariosta, I knew that for the first few weeks there were no guarantees that I would ever ride again.

I felt powerless. I've always been able to take care of myself, fight for myself, depend on myself. All of a sudden a lot of what was happening with my body wasn't up to me. My friends and fans kept my spirits from flagging. I received hundreds of cards, flowers, and balloons. The walls of my hospital room were covered. Cathy Clark brought me a smelly old horse brush so that I could inhale the rich, salty smell. So I wouldn't forget what I loved.

I have never had to depend so completely on other people. I had to open my hands and let the responsibility of my life slide into theirs. My fall at Saratoga put me in that position. I remember someone asking me at the Saratoga hospital where I wanted to have my surgeries performed, and by whom. I told that person I didn't want to have surgery. From that moment on, it was clear to everyone that I could not be counted on to make any decisions.

But my friends could, and they took over. My friends, the ones whom I never asked more than small favors of, because I didn't want to lean on anyone but myself, were there. And I knew that whether or not I'd ever ride again, they'd still be there. That was an amazing realization for me. That people loved me, not because I was Julie Krone, winning jockey, but because I am Julie Krone.

*   *   *

It was time to meet with the press, to tell them about my accident and prognosis for recovery. And, perhaps most difficult of all, to share with them, and with the thousands of fans who held my hand in their hearts during my surgeries and recuperation, my physical and emotional struggle to return to racing.

The day of my press conference (organized by Dan Leary at the hospital in Staten Island) I felt like a seven-year-old girl who had given out invitations to her birthday party and wondered if anyone would show. Prior to that conference, I had not spoken to many reporters. I had been in such agony that I could hardly talk to my mom and Paula, let alone answer the phone for interviews. In fact, I didn't even have a telephone, because it would have been useless.

When I was wheeled into the conference room, I was shocked to see it packed with reporters, photographers from the track, the guys who write the *Daily Racing Form* (track racing columns), and writers from the *New York Times*, the *Daily News* and the *Post*. Almost all my racetrack friends had come. I began to cry. It meant so much to me that people cared what had happened. Before the press conference I hadn't been sure that anyone would show; then to see all my friends in one group made me very emotional. And, for the first time, showing that emotion was all right with me.

Dr. Ariosta and I conducted the conference together. We made a great team. He told the reporters all the medical terms and prognosis, and I gave a lay person's account of what had happened to me. I told the truth. A few days later, I returned to my home in Colt's Neck, New Jersey, and began my painful rehabilitation.

The first time my physical therapist, Bob Bazley, looked at my ankle, he put on a serious, poker face. "Boy, that doesn't look too bad at all, Julie," he began. I looked at him and began to laugh. Later he told me that he had never seen such a damaged ankle but hadn't wanted to upset me. He needn't have worried; I knew it was bad. The skin on my ankle had been bandaged for so long that even the air hurt as it brushed the reddened and angry skin. Bob was very patient. In the beginning, my physical therapy simply involved exposing my skin to the air. Later we began to teach my muscles once again how to move my ankle. At first I could only move my big toe about an inch. Bob was encouraging, and slowly we began to work on moving my ankle from right to left. I improved quickly, but sometimes as I lay in the tub looking at my tiny left ankle and then glancing at the other ankle, a huge joint covered with black, blue, red, and yellow and lined with staples and scars, I grew disheartened. There also was still a lot of pain.

The pain was always there, but Bob was there, too, and so was Ken Mossman, my personal trainer. Ken is very talented, and was wonderfully creative with my workouts, since I could use only one leg. Ken knew just how much to push and when to give me a break. For the first few months everything went well. Then I fell into a dramatic depression.

It wasn't just that I couldn't ride, although that was definitely part of the reason. And it wasn't just that I was worried that perhaps I'd never ride again, or if so, not with my previous degree of success. It was the pain. I began to duck out of my physical therapy sessions and my workouts. Bob and Ken asked if they were doing something wrong. I told them no, it was just me. It took several more months before the pain became manageable enough for me to return to therapy. Still, it was always there.

In the middle of the night I would get up to go to the bathroom and forget that my right ankle was broken. I'd step on it and crumple in a heap of agony on the floor. It was humiliating for me. I've always been strong and able to take care of myself. I was the jockey who soaked my cast off when I broke my leg, and returned to the track four days later to win the meet at Monmouth. I was the kid who'd leapt from the roof of my family's barn. I'd been grown in the fields of Eau Claire, Michigan, and struggled against every type of prejudice to become a successful jockey. All of a sudden I was chained to a pair of crutches and burdened with a pain that I simply couldn't control.

I did a lot of soul-searching during the first few months of my recuperation. I spent time with my fears and weaknesses and learned not to hate myself for having them, showing them. And though the pain continued to haunt me, it was only in my ankle, not in my heart.

– 28 –

THE RETURN

I RARELY VISITED the racetrack during my eight-month recuperation. It was too painful to watch the horses go by, to remain rooted in the dirt while all the jockeys received a leg up and left the paddock to race. And while I could still feel the pounding *thhrrtt, thhrrtt, thhrrtt* through my shoes as powerful horses tore around the track, my spirit screamed That is not enough!

Two hundred and forty days after my spill at Saratoga I'd had enough of resting and healing — I wanted once again to feel complete. Several weeks earlier I'd called Scotty Schulhofer and asked if I could begin to gallop some of his horses. I knew that it would take at least a month of training before I was strong enough to ride races. Scotty agreed to let me gallop a few horses for him. On April 21, I drove the seventy-five miles from my home in New Jersey to Belmont Park.

What if I've lost all my talent? What if I'm not the rider I was before? What if no trainers want to ride me anymore? Those were the worries that plagued me as I drove to Belmont. For eight months I'd been riding a roller coaster of emotions. Constant pain had plunged me into depressions; family and friends had pulled me out. For some reason I thought that when I finally returned to racing the roller coaster would be over. I was wrong.

During my recuperation I had learned that highs and lows were part of my life — that each had to be experienced and appreciated. But it wasn't until that early morning drive that I accepted that my fears were also a part of my normal life. Regardless, as I left my car and headed toward Scotty's barn, I homed in on only one thought — Let's get this first day over with.

The press had the same idea. They were waiting for me at the track. I changed my clothes in the jocks' room and headed to the barn surrounded by the media and feeling at once flattered by their attention, slightly distracted, and a bit frightened. If I screwed up not only would I know, and Scotty and his foreman, Sal, but the entire world would watch me fail. It was extremely kind of Scotty and Sal to put up with the throng of media that flowed into their barn. Scotty runs a business, and the cameras and flashes disrupted his work and made some of the horses skittish. That day we were probably both wishing that my return could have been more low-key.

Sal picked two nice horses for me to gallop. The first was a sweet filly, Uncharted Waters. When I mounted, a flash scared her and she spun quickly. I remained tight in my seat. It felt natural to let my instincts begin to work, and I was glad that the filly wasn't completely calm. If a horse is always good, a jockey doesn't have the opportunity to tune her equine senses and reactions. Those senses are definitely brought out by race-horses, because of the high-strung atmosphere of racing and the horses' personality traits. I galloped the filly and then switched to a large male thoroughbred named Valval.

I hadn't galloped for so many months that when I was pounding around the track on Valval the exhilaration felt over-whelming. I can't believe I'm going this fast, I kept thinking to myself. When I dismounted, my exhaustion hit. Even though I'd been working out during my recuperation, there's nothing like riding. And it wasn't just that my grip got a bit tired — it's not really about strength like pulling, it's more about the strength to sit still, to not move for a long time. After my first day I realized I had a long way to go.

I was so sore the following morning that I had to roll on my side to put my socks on because my bum hurt so much. My legs, back, arms, shoulders, neck, and stomach were screaming. Every morning for the next few weeks I woke up and just had to laugh at the pain as I rolled out of bed and willed my body to spend another day training at the track. My focus was no longer solely on my ankle, though I did have to go though a process of trial and error in order to stabilize it and reduce the pain. The first problem was that the screws in my shin (I still had thirteen) protruded a bit, and I needed to put sponges in my boot so that the skin wasn't rubbed raw. Bob Bazley solved my second problem by giving me a brace that laces around my ankle to secure it. The brace has Velcro straps that crisscross over it so that my boot can slide on easily. Then there were my exercise boots, which are hard leather and lack the support of the tennis sneakers and sandals I'd been wearing for months.

Ariat, a boot manufacturer, went out of their way to make a boot that has a gel sole and a high arch that are very supportive.

Almost everyone and everything upon my return to the track was supportive. There were a few people that didn't react to my return the way I wished, but most of the powerful outfits that I had won for in the past wanted me again. Still, until the day when I returned to race riding, nothing could quiet the little voice inside that kept asking, What if I fall again?

Sooner or later every jockey falls from her horse. I knew that, I've always known that, and I'm one of those people who takes the risk. There's always been something inside me that allows me to say, "I'm gonna do this because I want to win." I believed that special drive could be recaptured, but I needed to race to show both myself and the world that I wasn't afraid to ride hard, to ride to win. I knew that it would take a while for my timing to come back, and I prayed that the trainers and my fans would be patient, would realize that I was still there giving a hundred and ten percent. I would never risk my life to do something halfway.

Deep breaths. That's what I told myself in order to stop shaking and quiet the five-hundred-pound butterflies in my stomach. Trainer Dick Dutrow had asked me to ride his horse Baypark on May 25 at Belmont. It was my first race since Saratoga, and as I sat in the jockeys' room part of me sang at the thought of riding racehorses again, while another part made my legs shake.

As I walked out of the jockeys' room and made my way to the paddock, my fans cheered and clapped. It felt wonderful to have them there to welcome me back. Mr. Dutrow acted the way he always does before a race, he put his arm around me and told me what to do as we walked toward Baypark. He was incredibly calm despite the television crews and flashing cameras, and I really appreciated him for putting up with the media attention and, most of all, for trusting me enough to put me back on my first horse.

The moment I mounted Baypark and headed for the track I stopped worrying about falling off. The excitement of finally being there shut out all other thoughts. Baypark was a kind horse, and he cantered properly in the post parade, hardly pulling me at all. He broke well from the starting gate and was laying third throughout the race. At one point I thought we were going to win, because in the middle of the turn I started pushing him and he picked up a bit. In the end we placed third. Baypark ran his best and I rode my best, so I felt good about the experience. I returned to the jockeys' room to wait for the eighth race, which I was riding aboard a horse named Life Boat. We finished eighth in that race. Still, I wasn't disheartened. I'd gotten that first day over with.

During those first two races I never thought that I was going to fall off my mounts. And as the day progressed I stopped having memories about crashing to the turf at Saratoga. Instead my thoughts shifted to how quickly a person's life can change. I've ridden thousands of races during my career, but one mistake, a split second of indecision, another jockey or horse, can change forever who I am both physically and emotionally. I guess that's something I had never thought too much about; it was something I had just accepted. Those thoughts were fleeting and quickly replaced with strategic thinking. Where do I want to place my horse, what do I have to do so that the continuity of the race allows my horse to win.

By the end of the day I knew that I still had work to do to regain more strength, but I also knew that Julie Krone was coming back.

Consider the Lily was also back. It was Lily's first race since her accident (which occurred on the same day as my own) had taken her out of racing for nine months. She returned to the track a week and a half after I did. And throughout my five weeks of training, she, too, was working toward her comeback. Al Jerkens, her trainer, began to let me ride her. Getting on her in the morning was a joy. She was all grown up, and though she still had all the cute characteristics I'd loved when she was a baby, especially her love of white grapes, now she was sharp and sassy. I felt myself regaining skills just as Lily felt her confidence returning. One afternoon Lily acted up while I was out talking to someone on the track. I sat tight and continued to talk, eventually feeling Lily relax to my touch. A trainer behind me was working with a jockey and his horse and I heard him say, "Boy, what a cocky little thing!" That made me feel good, because I realized that I was getting closer, that instead of thinking How am I going to ride? I was just reacting naturally.

Allen Jerkens scheduled Consider the Lily for an allowance race on May 26 at Belmont. I was named as the jockey. On the day of the race we broke from the gate and found ourselves in the lead. Lily was pretty anxious, but two hundred yards into the race I had her calmed, and we let two other horses, Hayley's Abby and Anthony's Pleasure, sprint past us. I wanted to conserve Lily's energy so that I could call on her in the stretch. The field of six racehorses pounded around the track — golden dust and streaks of red, blue, and green satin hit the shield of my goggles and were swept to the side. I focused on my horse, the race, the opportunity. We passed the half-mile pole and we were still lying third. I sat motionless, waiting for the right moment to push Lily forward. Hayley's Abby raced by the three-eighths pole, 660 yards from the wire. I waited. When Lily and I were 380 yards from the wire, I began to push her with my hands. We passed Hayley's Abby and held off Waving the Flag, ridden by Filiberto Leon (the jockey involved in my spill at Saratoga). We passed Waving the Flag at the one-eighth pole and finished ahead of Leon by a length and a half.

And there we were in the winner's circle. Me aboard my favorite dark bay filly, my trainer and friend Al Jerkens beside me, his smile telling me that all those months of pain had been worthwhile. My fans cheering, "You're back, Julie! You're back!" I dismounted and walked through the tunnel to the jockeys' room, all the colors and voices swirling in my head and clouding my eyes for a moment. Yes, I was back, but I finally understood that I had never been gone. And that the something inside me that always fought to win, that never gave in to the pain and that accepted no less than a hundred and ten percent, had never been gone either, because that something was simply me.